Into My Father's Wake

Eric Best

For Cardira –

Wisdom is where
you find it, and
you learn because
you are listening
for what you need.
Enjoy your journey!

Eric

© 2010 Eric Best

http://www.intomyfatherswake.com

ISBN-13: 978-1-449-97038-3

Printed in the United States of America

Acknowledgments

I would like to thank: my Godmother Mary Rousseau, who for more than 60 of her 93 years has encouraged me with the most unqualified love and support, and who kept asking me — for the last 20 years, "Had I finished yet?"; close friends who gave time and thoughtful energy to read early drafts and make suggestions, including Candida Donadio, Joan Goldsmith, Jeff Cook, Napier Collyns, Don Derosby, Jane Ganahl, Lori and Herb Colby, Pamela Bell; and my elder daughter Emily, who inspired much of what I wrote long ago and has since helped get it all into this form — and been a great sailing companion to boot;

In the practice and pursuit of writing: Fred Wagner, former chairman of the Hamilton College English Department, who taught me that so much writing is in the rewriting; Alex Haley, who insisted that I try to tell less and show more; and the late Albert Guerard and Macklin Bocock at the Stanford Writer's Program during and after my stay there in 1972-3, who urged me to keep going, no matter what; graduate school colleague and highly accomplished novelist Alice Hoffman for invaluable support she gave me so long ago that she has probably forgotten;

In the realm of boats and helping prepare Feo for what it takes to go to sea: Rick and Victoria Dawson, Gary Wheeler, Sheila Chandor and various supporters at Pier 39, Pineapple Sails in Oakland and the crew in the 1980s at San Francisco Boatworks in China Basin;

And most of all to my parents, Vincent and Katrina, both avid sailors, who gave me a start.

Contents

Into My Father's Wake

"We would rather be ruined than changed;
We would rather die in our dread
Than climb the cross of the moment
And let our illusions die."

W. H. Auden

Prologue

In the years before I finally went sailing alone I struggled with something nameless whose manifestation in my life I did not recognize for the longest time. Most of it was negative — a dull ache of some internal sort, sudden rage at conditions that would not submit to me, relationships that foundered in conflict or the effects of drinking, or drinking itself. This I had learned at home from a couple of experts and the traditions in which they came of age, where alcohol was just something one did at the end of the day. The drinking dulled but did not eliminate the background noise of the thing, which was perhaps the background noise of sadness, or echoes of irreconcilable conflicts, or the thing itself, whatever it might be. In matters of the heart, over time, I found I could only go so far and no farther, derailed or obstructed by something that must have been rooted in me early, if it was not my own by nature.

How much of this had to do with me alone and how much was a function of my family or the way I understood my place in it, or my father and mother, or the New England upbringing of my youth, I could not tell. It is easy enough to blame one's troubles on others, particularly the people who brought us into the world and raised us. But surely I figured in it somewhere. Who expected to be fully happy, anyway? Perhaps it was all in the pursuit, as books on the topic seemed to say. For a long time I did not appreciate that most people were not raised as I was, and therefore had their own experiences of parental love and the frailties and failures that went with it. Some of those were devious and for me would be intractable to understanding without the help of others.

Not until my first experiments with psychotherapy (in which I was the lone family explorer) with a grey-haired woman in Cambridge did I suspect there was something to uncover in my family that might explain some of my conflicts. Early school reports documented me as very clever and engaging, but contentious and sometimes explosive. My years growing up on a former dairy farm in a small Massachusetts town, and later in private schools, were marked by more than my share of fist-fights, confrontations on the soccer field and a record number of ice hockey penalties, though I never developed a taste for bar-brawls or street fighting. I could be very funny and entertaining — at least my family and friends generally said so — but when it came to being argumentative or provocative, few could match me in any grade from kindergarten on up. I despised authority in any form and if I felt the least bit trapped or pushed, in word or physical space, self-control was not my natural instinct. Call it spoiling for a fight, or a chip on his shoulder, or just a confused kid in pain, this tendency did little to endear me to my contemporaries, among whom I had a few but fortunately enduring friends.

If a turning point was signaled along the way it came without much notice during lunch in a Fifth Street bar in San Francisco in the mid '80s. I was in my mid-thirties, stunted in some ways I could not name, drinking regularly if not relentlessly and slipping inexorably into the collapse of my first marriage. I remarked to another journalist and unrequited novelist — bound together as we were by the San Francisco Examiner, our unrealized ambitions as writers and a common tendency to fly into rages over trivial matters — that I didn't think I could ever write my first book while my father was still alive. Why I said this at the time I was not sure, but I knew it was true and felt I was disclosing something powerful by saying it out loud to anyone. I was telling a truth without knowing why.

It would be about a decade before my father died in his waterfront bedroom in Cape Rosier, Maine, in the house my mother's father had built 80 years earlier, overlooking the rocky shores of Eggemoggin Reach, where I did my first sailing and my father did his last. In the meantime I had sailed alone to Hawaii and back and struggled to write the story of that trip and the life that brought me to it. Expecting his death by congestive heart failure to arrive at any time, I invited him to read the first draft, about which he only said, with a grim, narrow look I knew too well, 'So, you hate me, then?' It defined the gulf between us more eloquently than anything I could have ever come up with on my own. A few months later, with that still between us, I drove him home from the Bangor hospital, knowing it to be the last time, so he could have a view of the water and his sailboat, 'Enfin,' idling at her mooring nearby. He died three days later in his sleep, just after I left on a business trip. A dozen years would pass — including my mother's decline and death, and another failed marriage — before something moved me to finish the story once and for all — to try to accept and forgive and bury him with a decent tribute, and perhaps set myself free in ways I had never been.

It is a truism that we never know when we set out on a long journey just where we may arrive, or when. Life is made up of the unexpected, coming at us point-blank. Things are seldom what they seem, so our charted course is never the course we make in the end. While the father whom life dealt me left his indelible marks — for better and worse — there were others I found along the way. One was a tennis buddy of his, a former RAF pilot who flew night-fighters in Korea and then ran a mysterious business involving military hardware. During one of my explosive tantrums over a failed shot in a casual weekend doubles game, John Striebel looked at me with mild contempt and said simply, "That's it, I'm done." He sat down beside the court with an air of finality, rejecting summarily his younger partner, which broke up our precious Saturday game and made everyone a victim of my behavior. John was the first partner (or player) ever to walk off the tennis court when I was throwing a fit — the only one, actually. And I felt oddly grateful, even as I had to walk the half-mile home alone as he and my father drove past without showing any sign of my being there. Years later John would counsel me through my first divorce — don't let your anger take over, he said. He also warned me not to wait too long before trying to sail solo in the ocean. Getting older has a way of making you afraid to do things, he said, and the fear will come on you unexpectedly.

Other fathers I found, or who found me, helped me discover certain truths that I could not see clearly on my own. Don Michael, an educator and consultant who became a mentor to me in my consulting practice, looked at me with compassion when I recalled some of my earliest memories, some of them clouded or blocked, which had something to do with violence. "No child can reconcile love and brutality, it just doesn't make any sense," he said, putting me on a path to understanding my history over time. Joe Miller, a Sufi philosopher and spiritual guide in San Francisco, showed me the power of powerful listening and evoked words that would become my compass for the rest of my life. And Professor Bill White, who continued to teach through his last tortuous months at Harvard Business School as he died of leukemia, showed me with deathbed selflessness what it meant to help others find their way.

It was my own act of faith that in finishing this story something crucial about my father and my relationship to him might finally come clear, although its manifestation would be a surprise. The manuscript that had gone on the shelf after he died suddenly demanded attention when my son turned five. That was about the same age that I had become consciously aware that my father was in my life. He had spent my earliest years commuting from Connecticut to a New York City bank and was seldom at home when I was awake, a condition I had recreated in my own son's life. There was something about this age — five. My first daughter was five when my marriage to her mother broke up, and I felt compelled to get into the ocean alone, to get out there — maybe just to get out of here — to be truly alone to figure something out. This journey would not be finished, if I could call it so, for another 20 years. In truth perhaps it would never be.

I.

In The Path of My Fear

"To young men contemplating a voyage I would say go. The tales of rough usage are for the most part exaggerations, as also are the stories of sea danger... Dangers there are, to be sure, on the sea as well as on the land, but the intelligence and skill God gives to man reduce these to a minimum. And here comes in again the skillfully modeled ship worthy to sail the seas.

To face the elements is, to be sure, no light matter when the sea is in its grandest mood. You must then know the sea, and know that you know it, and not forget that it was made to be sailed over."

Joshua Slocum
Sailing Alone Around the World

I had known her first as a dream or perhaps an idea when I drove across the hot San Joaquin Valley floor in the days when I barely knew my first marriage would end, and came through the Valley of the Moon along the flat marshlands to the north of San Francisco Bay, swept down through the hills and riotous turns that lead into Sausalito, and walked the docks, alone but not aimlessly, with as much preoccupying my mind as troubling my heart. At least, that is the way I came to remember it, when time and experience had created such a filter to memory that I could only recall bare outlines and dim shadows of what I knew and when I knew it.

When I look back for intimations of my later departure, I see those walks in my late 20s, when life had brought me to those docks, or I had drifted there. Wood-spar sloops from Oregon and New England, fiberglass yachts scarred on Pacific coral, expansive dockside derelicts that did not know they had been abandoned to die, all waited there. Still I did not see her. I did not have an image in my thoughts as much as a feeling in my imagination that flew across the ceiling of my mind like a planetarium flashlight in search of a single star. If I held the flashlight then, I did not know it.

Who can say when an idea, born in dreams or embedded in the heart, first takes root, or how it stays alive, or why it struggles to endure? I walked the docks amid the breath-like rise and fall of hulls within slips, enveloped in the scent of the ocean at the land's edge, surrounded by bodies of small ships intimately wrapped in private quarters. The lines and textures of their hulls — white paint on wood, plastic shells polished to a sheen, aging timbers held by copper — hinted at their true nature, defined the quick and the durable, predicted survival or steadiness or the capacity for long passages through open water; partial ellipses and sheer curves, designs more rooted among marine life than man, hulls often voluptuous as they squatted or reclined. Above them rose a loose lace harbor fabric of infinite triangles, lines against more lines against halyards, stays and spars, all against the sky, and I lost myself. I lost myself to the unknown of where they had been that I had not, and where I might yet go with them.

She was there somewhere, I must have thought. Or she was at least somewhere even if she was not here. And yet I had no clear picture of her.

Feo first appeared in a photo stapled to a restaurant wall in China Basin, where the Todd Shipyards shoulder their way out into the Bay to embrace an occasional debilitated tanker.

"Joshua's sister-ship," read the small, typewritten caption. "Galvanized steel, central cockpit ketch. 47-feet LOA. 90,000 miles include a trip around the Horn. 2 heads, 8 berths, mahogany cabin."

Living alone in a small Potrero Hill cabin, I was newly separated from my eight-year marriage. A fresh scrap of paper carried calculations of how I could own a boat big enough to share with Emily, who would be with me on three out of four weekends a month, for Christmas holidays, and during the summers.

Feo was pictured in open water, all four sails set against a pearl white horizon. An array of white metal tubes seemed to be steering as three distant faces — two adults and a small child — smiled from the cockpit amidships.

"FEO" stood in foot-high capitals along her stern quarter, white letters on scarlet. The pale yellow deck and white cabin, its portholes gazing dispassionately out onto the water, caught the bright afternoon. Her double-ended design reminded me of a beach rescue boat crouched against the surf, equipped to take a beating and endure. The figure closest to me in the photo grinned through his beard.

"Self-steering autopilot, 9 sails, Yanmar diesel," the list went on. "Pier 39, Slip F-28."

❀

She moved heavily on the harbor swell. A large mechanical windlass leaked rust onto the foredeck. The cabin resembled a squat, rectangular gun turret welded onto the deck. Two thick masts pointed aloft like tall cannons supported by heavy wire stays. A bubble of clear plexiglas stared upwards from the cabin top like a single eye just ahead of the cockpit, which resembled a small foxhole, with narrow bench seats both sides and aft. Aluminum winches stood the forward corners and a spoked wheel was mounted thigh-high against the forward bulkhead. This steering station had an air of impregnability.

Just then a shirtless man appeared from an open hatch just aft of the cockpit. A hand-rolled cigarette hung from his lips and dark eyes dominated a bearded, salt and pepper face. He appeared to be in his late 40s but had the wiry, taut, muscular body of a man ten years younger.

"Hallo," he said. "Welcome to Feo." His accent suggested the south of France and too many cigarettes. He squinted at me as if searching for a distant buoy. "You are interested in her?"

"Yes."

A gesture told me to wait and he ducked out of sight.

I looked her over as I waited for him to reappear. The shape of her hull and the stoutness of her rigging contained all the courage I needed. A place from which to do battle. The city flowed down off Russian Hill and North Beach to join the restaurants and shops of Pier 39, a giant tentacle of commerce reaching north into the Bay. At this outer arm of the city the harbor resounded with ocean tempo from beyond the Gate.

If I could not accept the life I had, I could buy a boat whose nature held the potential of a voyage long imagined. My future would be built on the will to seize it.

The main hatch opened and the Frenchman reappeared to beckon me below.

"Michel," he said, and extended his hand in a fierce creature's grip. "Michel Riboni is my name. Entrez, please."

The paneling and floor of the main salon resembled an antique railroad car hollowed from dark mahogany logs. A wine-colored table stood in the center. Sunlight poured through two overhead hatches and portholes illuminated gold seat cushions along either side. A brass barometer and clock hung on the forward bulkhead with a pair of matching brass kerosene lanterns fixed port and starboard. French paperbacks jammed a long bookshelf behind a single bunk to starboard.

Michel moved nimbly about the salon, opening and closing compartments to demonstrate Feo's storage, or maybe just to give him something to do with his hands.

A navigator's berth extended aft under the port side. A section of cabin wall folded down onto the bunk to serve as a chart table, with a brass lamp, depth finder, speed gauge, and a panel of electric switches above, labeled in French. Opposite the companionway ladder a pair of stainless steel sinks and two-burner stove formed a right angle into a small tunnel.

"Sometimes at sea I can read two books a day," he said.

Brass-hinged doors opened onto the two-way radio, navigational journals and odds and ends along the port side. A narrow passageway led to a forward cabin and a pair of V-berths. The salon ceiling had been papered with aluminum foil.

"This is better for you in the tropics," he said.

He motioned me aft through the tunnel, between pantry shelves and the engine compartment, to the rear cabin. I had to bend over and twist slightly to get through, and I wondered how many new motions I would have to learn to live aboard.

The captain's cabin contained a double berth to port, another single to starboard. Small doors beneath a semicircle of five portholes concealed more equipment and clothes. A swinging door amidships exposed a grey diesel engine set deep in the bilge. A wooden ladder descending from the rear hatch opened out on a narrow door to reveal a toilet and porcelain washbasin behind it.

"You have your own bathroom here," he said proudly. "The shower is up there," he said, leading me back through the salon.

Just forward of the main cabin a small locker contained another toilet and faux marble sink. Someone had papered the tiny walls with Rubenesque nudes in black and white.

"Angelica's — how you say? — *idée de humeur,*" he said. "Sense of a joke. That is my wife for you."

I stepped into the forward cabin whose small floor between the V-berths allowed one person to stand and turn comfortably. Sunlight through an overhead hatch glowed orange and red in the cabin wood. Someone had papered the cabinets with animal stickers.

"African mahogany." Michel pulled up one cushion and opened a wood panel. "Inside this hull, there is no rust anywhere. *Rien.*"

Lanterns, tools, spare wire and rope, paint cans, sail remnants, sail bags, clothes, sacks of exotic seashells and a few child's toys jammed the compartment. I could see grey painted steel behind.

"You know the Joshua?" Michel began to roll another cigarette.

"No."

"Bernard Moitessier, he sail his Joshua, the first one, alone, nonstop, almost two times around the world. In the late '60s. You know his books?"

"No, I don't," I said.

"Aha. He wrote *The Long Way*. Bernard quit the first single-handed round-the-world race when he was far ahead. Competition was not the point, he said. *Life* is the point. He went on to Tahiti and did not come out for a long, long time." Michel uttered this in a tone of reverence.

I looked up from the navigator's berth through the bubble to passing clouds. A steering shaft poked through from the cockpit to connect to a small, spoked wheel inside at eye level. You could steer from here, peering out through the plexiglas bubble. Beneath the wheel were gauges for amperage and oil pressure and battery power.

"She is the strongest cruising boat in the Pacific right now," Michel said, from right behind me. "Not just because I want to sell her can I speak you this. You hit some steel container from fallen off a freighter and you don't sink, like a fiberglass boat can. And warm-water worms in tropics give you no worries."

He struck a match at the stove and blue flame appeared under the kettle.

"Coffee?"

I nodded.

In few moments there were two steaming cups on the table. Above, halyards ra-ta-tatted against the mast and dockside voices rose above the engine noise of a passing launch.

Michel had been a partner with his brother in a Geneva restaurant. When his marriage collapsed he had Feo built as a copy of Moitessier's and took her hull to be finished under his care in a Spanish boatyard, then set out to cross the Atlantic alone. Before that he had sailed only in lakes.

He brought her through the Canal, out to Hawaii and the Society Islands, down across the southern ocean and east around the Horn, still alone, then north to Rio de Janeiro, where he met Angelica. He had been solo then for six years.

They set sail together two days later. Not long after, his brother sold his share of the restaurant and two years later Michel's new partner quit sending money. Michel couldn't fight a Swiss court battle from Pacific atolls. He moved his hand elliptically and smoke from his cigarette rose like crooked tracings in the air.

"She has been very good to me. I am sailing one night at the Horn, reading, here." He pointed to the cabin light directly above.

"The tabletop is going like this — " His left arm rose and fell at the elbow like a drawbridge. "Up and down, up and down, up and down."

I saw how the table was hinged so it could fold in half, but might seat as many as six for dinner.

"Suddenly, boom! This huge noise! Now I am in there," he pointed to the bookshelf, "covered with books. When I crawl out, I am standing here."

He pointed to the floor.

"Water is coming in around my shoes. How can this be? Right then I bend over to undo the two screws by my feet."

He pointed up to the skylight hatch, held shut by a pair of butterfly nuts, and let out a brittle laugh.

"Ha- ha. I am standing on the water. The keel is over my head. We are upside down."

Michel stood up to mimic that position and I pictured him ankle-deep in books and water in the dark.

"Upside down?"

"Ah-ha, in a very bad place. You have air vents on the deck, you see, three forward, two aft. Where else does water come in, I am wondering? How long does the air last? Will she come upright? I am frozen with these thoughts, you know? Just then a big wave crashes the keel and she begins to come back. I had only the little sail up so the weight of the keel brings her back over. Outside, nothing is broken except the blade on the wind vane. I have plenty spares of those."

"Spare wind vanes?" I perceived his voice at a distance.

"Yes. You cannot steer all the time without her help. Always you bring extra vanes."

M y father listened as I worked the phone for several days from the house in Maine where I had come for two weeks, my first vacation since my divorce. I was going to buy this boat with no money — except a down payment that Michel agreed to loan me, and the rest from a bank, or so I thought. My father considered this creative financing and was curious to see how it would work. He had begun his career as a utility analyst at the Chase bank in New York in the 1920s and spent his last 30 years as a treasurer of a small-city natural gas company. It must have been obvious to him that no American bank was likely to lend $60,000 to a journalist on a 15-year-old French-built steel boat. Still, any boat loan in the post-Carter economy was worth about 11.5 percent a year, which my father considered an attractive rate.

I said I didn't want his help but preferred to do it on my own.

He shrugged. "Suit yourself. You won't find a bank with much taste for this. Besides, I know what you make and where to find you. I don't think you're going anywhere."

He was right about that, or most of it. There was no bank to be found willing to take the same risk on me that my father was, so after the fifteenth or twentieth fruitless phone call I grudgingly let him finance Feo. Michel and I concluded our negotiations by phone, and when I came down to her two weeks later as my own vessel — the first time I had owned anything significant without someone else involved — I discovered what it meant to feel proud and afraid.

A night breeze moaned from the northwest with the unique thrumming that wind can make through metal shrouds. Feo rose and fell on the harbor's movement like a large creature aware something much smaller had climbed onto her back. Standing in the cockpit with a sense of her mass under me, I stared up at the mast spreaders, stacked one above the other like twin crosses in the night sky, and tried to imagine Michel bidding her good-bye.

I pictured his angular figure someplace up the dock looking back at her, remembering all that had gone on between them across stretches of ocean and through remote islands that most could not even imagine. His "for sale" sign said 85,000 ocean miles, which was about two-and-a-half times around the world, but what had he seen? A hundred miles off the coast of Costa Rica, Angelica had been eight months pregnant when she developed appendicitis and they had to make a grueling, day-and-a-half sail upwind to medical help. Their daughter, Moemma, was born safely and by the time she came ashore with them as a wraith of a child in San Francisco seven years later she could trace all the major constellations in the stars, land big tuna on hand lines and imitate numerous South Sea dialects.

I tried to imagine his feelings as he approached the end of the pier, barely able to make out Feo's stout lines and heavy spars in the complex of distant rigging before finally losing sight of her.

"Welcome," said his note, penciled crudely onto a shipping tag. "I wish you fair winds."

A bouquet of dried flowers stood on the salon table. A tattered straw hat from some Pacific atoll shaded the overhead light. On a small inflatable globe of the world someone had drawn Michel's solo track in blue ink — down from Marseille and out the mouth of the Mediterranean, across the Atlantic and Pacific and South Pacific, doubling back around the Horn. From Rio the line turned red and made its way up and across through the Caribbean, through Panama to Baja, southwest to the Marquesas and New Caledonia. It meandered back through Vanua Levu and Christmas Island, touched Hawaii, and arced north through the world's largest expanse of open water before turning east to San Francisco.

I felt an intestinal rush as the idea leapt out into the cabin, a silent figure that contemplated me as I contemplated it. I did not estimate distance or try to imagine the difficulties. If I acknowledged too soon or too openly that I would attempt it, I might stumble over the fear of failure. I would prepare like someone keeping a secret from himself. There were things I had to learn: the basics of ocean navigation, the nature of Feo yet concealed.

Pillows cluttering the cabin released tiny feathers when touched. A carton of navigational charts dominated one of the forward berths. Moemma had abandoned a series of Mickey Mouse books in French and a stuffed chipmunk.

Now I saw her flaws. The gold cushions frayed along every edge. Screw-holes drilled here and there into the woodwork. Barometer glass cracked across its face, mended with tattered scotch tape. Electrical cords protruding like entrails from beneath the small refrigerator, which hummed and ticked like something about to expire. Sea water gurgled and stank in the forward head. In one storage bin after another lay odd tools, cables, shackles and sail-mending gear.

I opened up the envelope that stood beside the dried flowers and read Michel's cramped handwriting:

"Both heads, valves under sink must be closed if you use toilets. Pump hard and fast and it works like every other boat toilet, not well. Kitchen — left pump is soft water, right pump is salt water. It smell bad in harbor but use it at sea.

"Engine: Before to start, take off 1 oz. of fuel from the day tank to clean off rust and water; open water valve completely. Switch battery on (in the engine room). Start engine.

"When sailing, put a cork from wine bottle in hole where hand pump exhausts to avoid a return of water when beating against the wind with Feo heeled to port." He concluded:

"Be nice with Feo. I wish you the same beautiful time I had with her."

Waves of self-doubt rushed out like frightened live things into the confines of this steel shell. Gone was the world sailor who had cast a magic spell on me. How could I have bought my first boat without sailing her first? How could this tiny space become habitable? I knew nothing about boat electrics or old diesel engines.

Foghorns bleated in the distance. Music wafted down from the pier through the open porthole as the weight of permanence began to settle. She was mine now, for better or worse.

"Your second wife," my father had said, with a hint of sarcasm.

I had to expect these fears. I sat in the aft cabin, its double bunk like a beaver's lair in the rounded stern, and removed the lace curtains from the portholes.

Nothing had ever seemed more vast and irrevocable to me than to be in the ocean at night, alone with her sounds and concealed intentions. Some ancient balance of flesh and water and electricity, deep legacies of evolution, would absorb signals unknown to science. To sail across vast ocean reaches would be to rearrange myself from the inside and realign to the universe.

I clicked off the cabin light and listened to hull sounds in the water, faint lickings beneath.

I had promised myself to depart on an afternoon ebb tide and sail far enough offshore in the dark so I would not feel compelled to watch the land drop away behind. The returning flood tide would slow me down as I crossed the shipping lanes outside the mouth of San Francisco Bay, and I had been advised to get well beyond the procession of inbound and outbound freighters before nightfall.

Friends and neighbors came in a steady stream with home-baked cookies in shoeboxes, exotic Swiss candy bars, odd books and colored pencils, emergency gear, good wishes, talismans and advice. Nothing excites the Samaritan in people like the prospect of never seeing you again.

Pete, a veteran of Pacific crossings and a live-aboard neighbor, ambled over from his wooden ketch to contemplate the scattered boxes and tools and offshore gear that overran my cockpit. He held out a length of rubber surgical tubing and a small book, *Self-Steering for Sailboats*.

"You're gonna need these," he said.

"I've got extra vanes," I said. "I've got a spare for my spare."

"Sure you do. I appreciate that you went to college. Self-steering gear breaks. Mine did, on the way back from Hawaii with my wife and another kid. Few days of that and I could hardly stand up."

He pointed to the tubing.

"You'll need that stuff there. Nothing'll do like it." He chuckled in the small way that makes you aware someone is keeping the better part of a secret.

"Luck, too."

He watched in silence for a few minutes, and then backed away slowly.

"You need time by yourself, not people standing around like they're doing you some kind of favor. And remember — if things get bad, just heave to. Feo'll take care of you."

❖

The mahogany cabin lisped and ticked in the slip as I focused on final preparations. I had been warned that in the first days offshore, heavy northwest winds accelerating south around the Mendocino Coast would dislodge anything not secured in the cabin. Plastic packages of flashlight batteries went into a side compartment with medical supplies. Rolls of film and chocolates jammed a wire mesh basket dangling above the ice-chest. Books and personal journals, a radio-cassette player, a few dozen cassettes and an old pewter mug full of good luck charms overstuffed the starboard cabin shelf.

I tucked in a pair of leather-palmed gloves for handling wet lines in the cold. Moitessier's book, "The Long Way," warned against getting cuts on my fingers or hands. Salt-soaked cuts on your hand are the most common crippling injuries to anyone sailing alone at sea.

Something in my leaving provoked magical thinking in close friends. One delivered a boar's tooth, a porcupine quill, two black marbles and a tiny translucent opal fist from South America, symbols of strength and luck.

"I thought of you in Rio," she said. "Maybe this will help you sail to your realization."

A small ceramic Buddha, gift of a recent girlfriend who remembered my vivid dreams of drowning, now stood glued beneath a starboard porthole. Lockers in the main cabin held presents from my sister in Chicago, to be opened in numbered sequence along the way. A manila envelope bulged with 21 individual notes from Emily, exactly enough for three weeks.

"I can talk to you every day this way. You promise to read them?" The first was a green ballpoint outline of Feo atop a teetering wave. Beneath, her careful block lettering: "I love you, Feo and Dad."

Another close friend pressed a tin medallion into my hand, hexagon of robin's-egg blue embracing a scarlet circle with a silver circle inside. An Alaskan fisherman who possessed this charm had survived a storm in which all his crew-mates drowned, and he had given it to her.

"Let this be magical for you, too," said Sheila. "I know you will come back safely."

The final electrical connections completed, I walked up onto the Pier's upper level of restaurants for a Chinese dinner and sat where I could admire my now-working masthead lights. My fortune cookie said:

"You are about to travel to a faraway land that has long been in your waking thoughts."

I had never been more acutely aware of Feo than I was now, on the threshold of leaving. Months of planning and anticipation converged here, ready or not. In some ways I was not ready, and could never be. Fear of solitude had kept me from any journey in which I would be stripped of company, though I had long dreamed of a solo adventure of my own making. Fresh out of college I hatched a plan to ride on horseback from Massachusetts to the remote island where my father grew up in British Columbia. I would show up to my aging grandfather, who had taught horse mastership and boxing to British troops in India before war trauma sent him home a disturbed man, and my grandmother, a high Episcopal, missionary-nurse who raised her five sons — my father was the oldest — in the village of Ganges on Saltspring Island in the days before electricity or running water. My older brother had passed along stories gleaned from one of our Canadian cousins about how my father and the other boys tried to protect their mother during the old man's periodic attempts to shoot her with a .22-caliber rifle. Cap had accused her of producing their fifth son with an-other man, which was absurd once you saw how perfectly all five boys resembled each other. By the time my father reached his teens his mother had banished Cap to a separate cabin on the property, where he lived out their 65-year marriage to the bitter end.

But for reasons that loomed more important at the time, I ignored the voice that urged me to cross the continent alone and instead, with a girlfriend following in my VW, drove a mo-torcycle across the trans-Canada Highway to the Stanford Uni-versity writers program.

"If you really want to be a writer," my father said at the time, "Why don't you just sit down somewhere and do it?"

The moment of stepping aboard Feo for the last time before shoving off brought with it the drained and vaguely para-lyzed sensation I felt whenever I found myself at any significant height above the ground. Physical strength seemed to pour out the bottom of me and now my hands fumbled with the hatch.

Alone at last, I was truly afraid.

What if I got lost? I planned to learn celestial navigation en route. Others had done the same, without the directional guidance of Loran, which promised to correct my calculations going offshore until I knew what I was doing with the sextant and its workbooks. Maybe the Loran would deceive me on the approach to the islands, as some sailors complained it had, be-cause Hawaii lacked adequate signal towers to produce a reliable fix. But maybe small errors would accumulate to lead me astray, or one wrong calculation would cause me to miss that tiny collection of islands in mid-ocean.

Plenty of sailors had been successful alone in the ocean. Just before the turn of the century, Joshua Slocum had circumnavigated the world in his 37-foot Spray, a beamy sloop with no engine and far fewer maritime aids, although the ocean had been his life for more than 30 years and contemporary dangers had not developed yet. Tanker traffic was negligible. In Slocum's day, steel containers the size of boxcars did not fall off ships to float like miniature icebergs, mostly submerged and deadly to small hulls passing by.

The famous solo sailors from the late 60s like Eric Tabarly and Moitessier and Robin Knox-Johnson, who competed in the first round-the-world single-handed race, survived the toughest ocean conditions to tell about it. Eric Chichester had made his fame with a non-stop solo sail at age 65. Plenty of people, older and younger than I was, had done tougher solo sails than the one I was facing now. I reassured myself that any competent small-boat sailor in reasonable physical condition could sail a proven ketch like Feo halfway across the Pacific alone even if he never had done anything like it before.

"You're out of your mind," my father said when I first disclosed my intention. "You haven't sailed enough in the open ocean. You call this prudent?" His tone mixed skepticism with contempt. I would be relying on small-boat sailing as a boy and coastal cruising with him almost 25 years before. I had never sailed through anything longer or more violent than a passing thunder squall, nor piloted myself in thick fog. I had never been into the deep ocean and still had fewer than three weeks of sailing Feo in San Francisco Bay, which my father pointed out several times. He was quick to point out flaws or weaknesses of any kind, and his pale blue eyes could bore in like a laser as he did so, which I could see even when he reiterated all this by telephone as my departure day drew near.

Mid-June was supposed to be the ideal fair-weather window for the crossing, but hurricanes were known to sweep from Mexico to Hawaii in July and August with little warning. What if I lost the rigging? I had no experience reading offshore Pacific cloud patterns and only knew the ocean's nature by anecdote and reputation.

This is the safest time to go.

I had been about eight years old when I first sailed the family's little sloop in Maine, an all-wood Herreshoff design with a salmon-colored half-deck forward and a cockpit the shape of a walnut shell. Its mast and boom were no thicker than my father's forearm and the tiller fit in my hand like the handle of a hammer. My mother's father had it built for her and her two sisters in the 1920s and my brother and sister and I would all learn to sail it among the islands just west of Little Deer Isle in Penobscot Bay. The youngest of the three of us, I was the most devoted to it, just as my father had been "the only one of my boys who ever cared more for sailing than shooting," my grandmother said. And my mother would eventually say that the two of us "would just about sail anything in anything."

My mother's voice in the earliest days would resound from the porch of the house, and sometimes she came all the way down the runway from the porch to the gangplank above the dock to yell at me to "stay inside the circle!" She meant Barney's Ledge and Buck Island and Spectacle Island, a trio of up-croppings of rock and scrub grass and a few pines that described an arc just offshore from the house that gave me about a square mile in which to maneuver. The wind could pipe up suddenly from the south, or squalls could come barreling off the high ground of Cape Rosier and whip through Weir Cove in sudden treacherous bursts, and my Grandfather Prentice's first and perhaps only law of sailing would ring in my ears:

"If you wonder if it's time to reef — it's time to reef!"

I learned as a child does before words are put on experience that the sea has a mind of her own and will not be denied. Sinister tones of grey could develop quickly to the southeast and stacked clouds above the land could mean sudden squalls coming. When salt scent replaced pine in the wind or the temperature fell sharply, you ran for home. On the 36-foot sloop *Candida*, a race-built Geiger design loaned to my father by a close friend to cruise the New England shore in the summer, a stiff breeze could cant the deck as steep as a stairway and strike terror into any small, unprepared heart. But Candida would not tip over if you spilled wind from her sails as she heeled, my father showed us, or turned the bow up into the gust or released the mainsail sheet that held the boom tight against the wind. Any of these moves, or a combination, would render the most powerful gust harmless — if you were quick enough. My father taught that you survived by knowing your boat and respecting the elements, and anticipation was always the best part of common sense, and the true meaning of first aid.

Gus, the ex-Coast Guard officer and navigation instructor in Alameda, where many San Francisco sailors went for navigation training, had hammered the rudiments of coastal piloting into our winter's class of amateurs, some of who were planning ocean passages like mine.

"The sea lies in wait for the unwary, but she stalks the reckless," he said. One eye slightly askew and bushy eyebrows awry, he fixed us in his cockeyed stare and let those words sink in. *She stalks the reckless.* Offshore, he said, be prepared for everything — and assume nothing.

Sailors who had raced the single-handed Transpac event across the 2,400 miles to Hawaii in early summer admitted to fears of freighters, being becalmed in the doldrums or miscalculating their positions en route to the islands and missing them altogether. Those who had competed even once — and many were repeaters — were rich in survival tips, which I researched like any journeyman journalist preparing for a story.

"It takes a tanker less than 20 minutes from the time it appears until it's on top of you," said one. "Astonishing how fast they gallop over the horizon."

He had come up into his cockpit from cooking waffles down below to see a Panamanian ship looming above and flung the helm over just in time for a great steel wall of barnacles to scrape by. His radar detector had sounded no alarm, and he saw no sign of anyone aboard as the freighter cruised on by.

Who knew how many sailboats disappeared under cargo ships that had no one on lookout and would not even notice the collision, day or night?

Calms could drive you crazy in a few days, your nerves shot by slatting sails. Eggshells thrown overboard at night would still be floating alongside the next morning. Sudden night squalls caught you in the dark with too much canvas up because you were too tired or lazy to shorten the sails down for the night.

"I put the bloody sails up and figure God'll take'm down," said one veteran. "He always does, bless'im."

Between food and sleep, the first priority is sleep. The boat will tell you when she needs help.

Don't rely on Loran. Never trust shore lights and never enter a Hawaiian harbor at night. Get your celestial calculations down pat. They are your fail-safe. Never go on deck without your harness. Never. Sleep in it.

It required no ocean background to know that falling overboard alone would be a fatal event. I had never handled sails while wearing a harness. Two lines attached to a steel ring at my chest would be clipped into the rigging or to the jacklines that ran along the deck from bow to stern. To a beginner this felt like a sure-fire recipe for tripping oneself up.

What if I were injured and unable to call for help? The EPIRB, a battery-fed device that could transmit Feo's distress position to passing aircraft, would be useless if there were no one there to flip it on.

O n this afternoon in mid-June, San Francisco Bay burned westward under cloud-bent sun, a pathway almost too dazzling to face. Vibration rose from the cockpit floor as Feo's burbling exhaust at the waterline mixed smoke and steam and sound in equal parts. Distracted by an overtaking fuel tanker that suddenly appeared around the southeast corner of the city front, I didn't think much about the smoke in the exhaust at the time.

The freighter loomed black like a windowless skyscraper churning along on its side, pushing a white bow-wave ahead like giant V-shaped roller to ease its progress. The deck was dead flat with silver fuel pipes and dark valves interwoven back to the white control tower astern, a solid cube as wide and tall as the ship itself. A row of windows stared like the baleful eyes of some Neanderthal. It stretched the length of two football fields, black turning to rust-red above the waterline, sign of a high-riding, empty hold. Her name was *Pena Vento*.

She ran the several miles of city waterfront in just a few minutes, past the glassy repetitive downtown office towers, past the Big Ben clock at the Ferry Building showing half-past two, past Chinatown porticoes and Telegraph Hill, past the Italian stucco of North Beach balconies and the slate roofs of the Marina district, and finally the hairline grey beach and forests of the Presidio, anachronistic military defender of the Bay entrance. The tanker seemed to gather up the city skyline and everything in it, to draw all things settled and civilized into the spot where the Golden Gate now hung, faint thread of an arch between two distant points of land, pursed mouth of the great horseshoe and final portal toward which Feo and I were now aimed as well.

In a shaft of afternoon light the ocean chart shone white and yellow from the salon table. Across the expanse of four million square miles stretched my course of dark ink, parallel to the Alaskan Peninsula, straight from the Farallon Islands a few miles northwest of the Gate, whose rocky up-cropping I hoped to clear by nightfall, to Oahu.

❀

The old man would be sitting on that porch in Maine by now. I could picture his vivid white thatch of thinning hair, bushy eyebrows above blue-grey eyes and a rugby-damaged nose, clipped grey moustache and that perpetually clenching and unclenching jaw muscle. His stoic British face stared out east across Penobscot Bay, fallen into darkness and empty of the sailboats that plied it on a clear summer day. "Enfin," the 18-foot sloop he gave himself as a retirement present, would be idle at her mooring. He would no longer go down to her alone since a recent fall overboard, when he nearly drowned.

I imagined bringing him along for one last long sail and for the kind of time alone we had made too little of in our lives, almost always on boats, when we got along so well with each other. On board a boat — any boat — he lost that clenched intensity. A relaxation overtook his body that flowed into his voice and it seemed the only place — except for the ski slope or the dance floor — where he was at peace with himself and others. He only brought close friends, he commanded the space with ease, and there was no hint of cruelty in his discipline.

Alcatraz had crept up and passed to the south like a stone supertanker inbound, its light flashing at six-second intervals. The prison tower faded away into the distant city skyline. The Golden Gate rose ahead, straight-legged giant of a bronze insect straddling precipitous shores. Once through it, we would be on our way, to venture for the first time into the ocean and to cross two-thirds the width of the United States, as the frigate bird flies, alone.

I could picture him, slightly crouched with me in this cockpit, balanced as a dancer against the movement of the ocean, same tattered tennis cap perched on his head to ward off skin cancer. His gifted eyes, the first always to spot distant buoys, would be drawn again and again to the horizon. He would use the sextant he had given me for this trip to finally learn to reduce the sun's angle to a precise position, something he often spoke of whenever we were on the water together but never got around to. I would make hot drinks to stave off the night chill and let him age gently, breathing the pure Pacific air of his youth.

Feo drew herself up on incoming ocean swells as she passed between the bridge towers. I pictured his head cocking upwards as the Gate swept uproariously over and a deluge of rush-hour traffic noise filled the air.

He would know the smell and rhythm of this ocean and feel returned to the coast of his boyhood, where the sun sets over water.

In a dream I had just a few nights before leaving, he and Emily sailed off into the night with me and holes appeared in the hull underwater, where green water began to flood in. *Quick, where were the epoxy and the plugs?* I could not see the leaks or get far enough down in the hold to find the source.

The swirl of out-flowing green stretched to ocean rollers piling above Potato Patch Shoal a mile ahead. Distant mottled water matched the overcast. Grey clouds struck the land to starboard and overran the Marin headlands, whose conical mounds rose sharply to the north and the shrubbery seemed to cascade off dark cliffs into the ocean.

He would gaze to the Pacific northwest of his earliest sailing and sense before I did the wind coming up.

At exactly 6:07:15 PST, the bridge passed overhead. I expected to feel something dramatic exiting the Gate, with 2,400 open-ocean miles to the next landfall. This plunge — to get myself free and clear — now abandoned any last tethering point. There was no turning back from the open water, where there was no listener, no father-savior, no one watching. If and when I arrived in Hawaii, I felt sure I would never be the same.

The stiff white canvas of the new mainsail chafed audibly under bright red lashings. Lifelines running knee-high and taut between stanchions every few feet along the gunwales promised to help keep me aboard in the roughest conditions that might come. The staunch mast, which I had stripped and sanded and repainted in recent months, gleamed like an oval shaft of ivory. The wind telltale perched jauntily on the top and pointed its fluorescent orange beak to the sunset.

If Feo went down, how easily could I cut the dinghy free and launch it over the side? Within the pulpit, the flapping figure of the jib shrugged off the mild westerly and craned after the Pena Vento, now a vanishing speck to the southwest.

T he U.S. Coastal Pilot for the North Pacific makes the route to Oahu sound straightforward and simple.

"Follow San Francisco Traffic Separation Scheme route to a position south of Farallon Islands, thence rhumb (straight) line to: Twenty-one degrees, 14 minutes North; 157 degrees, 39 minutes West."

This neglects to mention the Pacific high-pressure system. This is a meteorological doughnut off the continent where winds blow clockwise around a center of calm, shifting unpredictably north and south throughout the summer. This uncertainty induces many sailors to aim beneath the doughnut, looking for reliable north-easterlies and warmer temperatures. Others take their chances that the rhumb line must be the quickest course between two points, whatever winds and calms may occur along that path.

A catamaran skipper preparing for the Transpacific Race to Hawaii scoffed that too many competitors sail hundreds of extra miles to avoid the high, only to be overtaken by it anyway.

"I take the rhumb line and sail to the weather the way I see it. Just be prepared to change your plan," he said.

A whale broached between his pontoons a few weeks later and the catamaran went down in thirty minutes. Only the quick arrival of a nearby racer saved him.

The wiry little man who taught celestial navigation for the Bay Oceanic Society had left San Francisco for Hawaii one summer with a few navigation books and a sextant, never having plotted an ocean position before, and showed up in Honolulu three weeks later. Celestial Sam, as he liked to be known, put forth his own solo voyage as an example any student might follow. Whether he was aided by his three decades as a state road surveyor I do not know.

"Just go south 'til the butter melts," he said. "Then go west 'til you hear ukuleles on the radio."

My plan was to leave the Farallon Islands lighthouse to starboard and take the rhumb line to Oahu. For the first few hundred miles, gales were common. Then the wind was expected to moderate and shift east as we bore southwest. The Pilot Chart of the North Pacific showed a knot of current pushing that way. If the high pressure system overtook me, I figured I could motor through the calm patch in a day or two.

I did not know what to expect where wind and waves had driven across thousands of open ocean miles. I had never been prone to seasickness, but a few days of ocean swells or storm conditions in a closed cabin might change that. I had been violently sick only once onboard Candida when I was about eight years old, after splitting a package of Oreo cookies with my older sister, who had thrown up just minutes before I did. My father watched my masticated Oreos disappear over the side and then bundled me into the cockpit, where he shielded me from the wind and promised the fresh air would cure me.

"Beautiful thing about seasickness," he said, "Once is enough. You will never, ever, be seasick again." When he said things in his particular tone of authority I had no choice but to believe them. And I had never been seasick again, even in rough weather inside Cape Cod during a particularly nasty southerly when I was about 12.

Be prepared to stay awake the first several days, possibly the worst. Constipation, diarrhea and nausea are common. Stay warm. Hypothermia is deadly, you may not recover after your judgment goes.

With twilight fading and the hot smell of diesel rising into the cockpit, I shut off the motor, tugged the main down and let Feo meander west between the shipping corridors. I had been staring into the oncoming night, nagged by one major chore left undone.

A year before, I'd laid up Feo's mast in the boat yard, stripped its fittings and sanded it smooth. I cut and fit new spreaders, filled a few rotten spots, and repainted the spar top to bottom. But when I replaced the mainsail track to carry the sail upon its slides, I created one zig-zag joint between sections where they should have lain perfectly straight. It was a treacherous sticking point for the slides that would not go away. *Nothing is more lethal than a big sail that refuses to come down.*

Now as the wind went shifty and feeble the open ocean forced me to confront the crooked sail-track or leave it, a dangerous sticking point if the weather ever got ugly before I could get the sail down. As I crouched on deck with the mainsail in my lap and sand-papered the corners of each track slide, a Toyota-emblazoned freighter surged out of the Gate. The sun had fallen almost to the horizon, encircled by a blurred, rose-colored ring. Feo's demands replaced the anxieties that had gripped me. I could not afford to get caught with too much sail up.

Eat before you get light-headed, sleep before exhaustion. Keep a close watch! Don't leave the helm unattended for long.

By the time I had re-hoisted the main, Feo had retreated on the incoming tide toward the heart of freighter traffic. The ridge descending northwest from Mt. Tamalpais looked like a bearded man lying asleep on his back, hands folded on his chest. His forehead became Pt. Bonita as I approached its dolorous offshore bell.

"Clang-bong...Clang-bong....clang...clang...Clang-bong..."

Dusk turned the ocean to woven metal. The bell faded into the noise of engine and hull and night came down. With it came a sense that with this final up-cropping of continent I would leave my life behind, as much as one ever could. I would rely on Feo and heed the words passed down:

If you wonder if it's time to reef, it's time to reef. When things get really bad, you can always heave to.

In perfect daylight from the deck of a 40-foot sailboat you can see an object on the water about four miles away. But lights in the dark at sea have the illusory quality of mirage, with no horizon or reference to suggest relative distance. What appears to blink may in reality be a steady light interrupted by waves breaking onshore or by a rollers rising somewhere in between. What you thought was a fixed red buoy of a distant harbor marker suddenly becomes the port (left-side) light of a fishing boat, bobbing nearby.

Hunched in the cockpit and squinting at pinpoints of two freighters converging from the northwest on San Francisco, I gave up any hope of sleep. I could see no lights on either freighter to define their angles of approach. Did these pinpoints of light enlarge, minute by minute, or did I stare at them with such intensity they seemed to enlarge? Were they approaching head-on, or passing safely? I stood riveted at the wheel, mindful of Feo's weak progress against the headwinds and incoming tide.

Seen through the binoculars, one might be a man walking with a candle, faint flame rocking. Were those faint outlines a ship's deck? *The lights of one are white, then green. No, one is white, another green. I cannot be sure.*

If only the green starboard running light of the ship is visible on approach, then the ship must be passing left to right. A single white light with a green light clearly to the left and red to the right means the ship must be coming at me.

If a ship remains on the same compass heading from you while you maintain your course, the two of you are on a collision course. If you misjudge at close range and turn when they turn, your error may be irrevocable, an error that analysis of ship collisions has shown to be oddly common. Somewhere near this spot in evening fog not long ago the crew of the fishing trawler *Jack Junior* shrieked its position into Channel 16 as the cargo vessel *Golden Gate* plowed through them — a fatal collision the freighter operators later tried to conceal. The lights might have been invisible, or seemed far away, then revealed themselves to be too close, inescapable at the last.

They would run you down and lie about it later.

Below in the eerie glow of one overhead cabin light, I clutched the two-way radio.

"Feo on Channel 16 to any freighter in vicinity. Any freighter! Do you read me? Over?"

My ridiculously small masthead light is camouflaged against shoreline lights. They might see red and green on Feo's deck if they happened to be looking and if their own massively tall bow did not block the helmsman's view.

No answer.

My steaming light midway up the mast illuminates the staysail. The bright triangle makes me easier for them to see but effectively blinds me with its glare to everything ahead. I flick the light on and off several times, then leave it off. They know I have to get out of their way. They are in the traffic separation zones meant for tankers and I am in neutral waters. A bright blip on their radar would show Feo's solid steel, impossible to miss. We must be safe.

Maybe their radar has failed to detect me, or I don't know where I am.

"Feo to any freighter in the vicinity north channel zone. Over!"

No answer.

Why am I down below when they are closing in?

I climb back up into the cockpit, expecting a monstrous hull on approach. The pinpoints in the distance continue to converge.

Are they?

I jump down below again and duck through the tunnel to the engine room door. Open the salt water cooling valve and hit the main power switch. Press the starter button. The engine wheels to life. Feo surges ahead with a hiss and shudder on a course that will drive us between these converging lights.

Suddenly the diesel's chugging runs gently off downhill and away, turning up at the end into a wheeze. *Pee-shaw!*

Then nothing.

Why now, with two freighters coming on in the dark? Have I come only this far to be run down?

I jump below again. The engine catches immediately and rumbles thickly on. A bubble of water somewhere in the diesel line — that was it!

The faint smell of oil rises again. In the dark of the engine room, something grey waved in the beam of my flashlight.

By now the tanker lights to the north have moved perceptibly south. The westerly pinpoints are fading, false threat. The tankers will easily pass at a distance. I have humiliated myself on the radio.

*I*n a session with Brody, the Berkeley shrink I began to see soon after my illness, I had written: mother/ sister/ lovers/ women/ wives. I had never tried to get all of that by the throat.

Now my behavior is doing that, I said.

What you're doing now? Brody said. He had a way of repeating the last thing I said, like a police detective who wants all the information to flow in one direction.

Yes. You asked me how I respond to women getting angry at me. I wrote down a list of women I have loved, and thought, what is it? What was the relationship, where did it go, where is it now? I saw some things come up.

Some things? Brody said.

A relationship would start — crack! Very intensely. I would pour myself into it 110 percent. It would come to a certain point and then pretty much stop. I mean stop. End. Stop. So now I say this is a pattern, but what is this pattern? I don't want this pattern.

This pattern? echoed Brody.

In my journals I see someone struggling for something.

That's what you see when you look at yourself, you see someone struggling? Brody asked.

What I think is that if someone's self esteem is low, they look for esteem from the outside. They don't believe in their own achievements. Maybe because I don't love me, I seek someone to love me. But if I don't love me, then nothing will last. I can probably get someone to love me by turning all of myself on to them. Then because I don't deserve what comes back, I feel guilty. So I begin to look for imperfection. And when I find enough imperfection, the woman doesn't have adequate standing anymore. Now I feel pretty shitty about myself.

Where does that feeling come from, feeling shitty about yourself?

You've accepted my analysis?

If you want me to, he said.

A good friend of mine asked me what was I really insecure about? In the back room of my soul, let's call it, some internal presence shrieks at me for making mistakes, hates me, abuses me, won't let me alone, won't help. Just attacks. As long as I can remember that voice treats me in a way I would never let another human being treat me. I'm in some kind of battle to get in command, to believe in myself, that I am not just a collection of incoherent, conflicted feelings, not knowing which one is me. I don't need that anymore.

The voice on the tape was faint, depressed, disheartened.

D etachment came swiftly beyond Farallon Light, 358 feet above the water on a 41-foot tower, outermost beacon of the coast here. The light had not come up off the starboard bow as I expected, a gradual winking from the horizon and steady approach, but loomed as a sudden giant blade in the night mist, prison spotlight revolving overhead in pursuit of escapees. I had not known I was even close to it.

The light and uncertainty and fear arrived simultaneously. I turned Feo sharply left and south. The tower inched across the black to my right shoulder. As it drew abeam I wasn't sure whether I would clear the unlighted rock the chart showed to be a quarter mile south of the tower.

It hit me then: I did not know exactly where I was, or not exactly enough.

The air choked with the sound of wind in the shrouds and waves rushing past Feo. I turned my head from side to side and craned my ears to catch any surf-like sound above the engine noise, any interruption in the wash and re-wash of waves coursing around me to suggest rocks breaking the surface nearby.

Nothing appeared in all that perfect darkness except the faint lines of the boom and sails, the fluorescent beak of the tell-tale atop the mast and the scudding mist that raced past the glow of its little light. If I shined my flashlight in the cockpit, the small pale circle contained just my body. Everything I had been able to make out a moment before — Feo's bow and the vane behind, my sense of her boundaries — dropped away. Turning on the flashlight illuminated my perfect isolation, so I turned it off and let my senses expand into the night. After a while, as the tower light receded astern, we were not so much in the dark as of it.

Joe Miller waited at the top of a long flight of wooden stairs in the Nob Hill apartment that had been a lifetime gift to him from the San Francisco Theosophical Society.

Bright bald forehead. Fringe of white hair. Angular cheekbones, imposing nose and a sharp white goatee. Small head atop a thin neck.

Joe smiled at me through evident pain from a recently broken hip, and his glittering blue eyes reminded me of the Rime of the Ancient Mariner, the transfixing look of the story-teller.

He embraced me in the right cheek to right cheek, left cheek to left cheek manner of Sufis, and beckoned me into his sitting room overlooking Stockton Street. He held his wiry, sprightly body slightly akimbo, gestured to an easy chair, then sat down carefully to face me.

"You have been quite ill, I understand?" he said.

"Yes. I never felt close to death before," I said.

Joe began to talk about illness as a sign of emotions, un-cried tears perhaps. Then he waited for me. He listened in a way I had not experienced before from any friend or therapist and certainly not from my family. His listening seemed to descend from the level of his eyes and ears to his chest and rib-cage, and he sat like an open receptor, not judging, not waiting to speak. Just taking it all in.

I told him about my most vivid dream from my early 20s in Bath, England, a vision of my own migration along a remote mountain path. The walk was composed of solitary arrivals and departures, in one small village after another. Each time I did not want to leave but felt compelled. Always without company. Some touched me with their hands as I departed. Were they people I met or would yet know? Actual villages? I did not know whether to pursue them as real destinations or abandon them.

"You were extremely ill just now, your friend told me," Joe said suddenly, as if to bring me back.

"Yes."

The promotion to metro editor, for which I had originally come to the Examiner from the city editor's job in Stockton, had gone to someone else. My customary winter flu turned suddenly to pneumonia and within a few hours of the news I collapsed on a sidewalk and had to be taken to the hospital by ambulance. Pleurisy. My father had it once and said it felt like a knife in the back. Now I knew what he was talking about.

The doctor asked me (rhetorically, it seemed) why a person of my age in good physical shape would fall so ill at a simple career disappointment? He suggested a psychotherapist named Brody in the East Bay. Maybe it would be useful to talk to a man about my own age. I did not really want to see another psychiatrist, which I had tried several times during my failing marriage. But I still didn't know whatever it was I needed to understand. So I agreed to try again. And a close friend of mine, a New York Jew who turned to Sufism during the Flower generation years, suggested this audience with Joe, an elder with whom he went on periodic contemplative walks in Golden Gate Park.

I told Joe now about the therapist in Stockton a few years before who urged me to confront my father. I was about to go home for a holiday visit and predicted his drinking and rage would repeat itself, as it always did, and suck me into their scene all over again.

"If you would have it change with him, who would do it?" the therapist had asked me. "Will your father do it?" He left this question in the air for me to answer and it all seemed obvious. If anything were to change between us it would have to come from me.

Another therapist had shot back an arrow of my own words from the corner of her Danish enclave overlooking the Charles River when I suggested maybe I did not want to be married after all.

"Yes, maybe you do not want to be married at all."

Her eyes narrowed when I described how my mother would banish me to my room to wait for my father's brand of whipping, how he would come upstairs with great deliberation to use the hose, expertly, maybe from before I could remember. I did not want to find excuses for myself in past experience.

Sometimes I felt there was something stuck inside me, something larger than my own body trying to get out. The prospect of its exit could bring me to violent trembling, as if the thing upon exit would split me open and break me apart. Like trying to vomit a truck, I said. It would kill me if it came out or eat me up more slowly if I kept it in.

Now it began moving up into my throat and Joe watched me convulse around it, choking it back, fighting to remain silent.

"What is it, then?" he said kindly.

"I don't know," I said. I could hear a rushing sound and felt myself concentrating my eyes on a small oil spot on the floor. Whenever my mind asked, an answer rose inchoate, inarticulate. A sick feeling. Bigger than I was. Grief, awaiting release.

"You are a man with considerable abilities and you have thought about this for a long time," Joe said. "I wonder — if you came to you with what is in you now, what counsel would you give to yourself?"

An answer leaped out even though this question had never been put to me:

"I would tell me to live closer to my heart and walk in the path of my fear," I said.

"Ah." Joe tipped his head back, his white goatee aimed at my chest. "I understand the first part. What do you mean by the second?"

I had been reading *The Sleeping Beauty* to Emily. The dwarf's advice to the Prince was: walk toward the thing you fear most and it will disappear before you reach it. Bound up in a tale retold to generations of children, this admonition hit me clearly for the first time.

Your fear should be the path.

Joe smiled. Raindrops striking the windowpanes behind him collected as luminescent beads on the glass. In a nearby room his wife began to play the piano.

"Most people do not walk toward their fears," he said.

"Do most people know what they are?"

"Do you?"

My mother disappeared at the end of a shining corridor that smelled of wax and tile. Women in starched white, insect-shaped, were crisscrossing the hallway, holding sheets. Her heels click-clacked into the far end until I could only see the glint of her shoes against a far doorway. The horizontal railing around my bed pressed against my chest. My small voice rose in pursuit of her into the darkness. She was gone. It was the early 50s in Massachusetts and the Lowell General Hospital feared a polio epidemic.

"I think I am afraid to be alone."

"Most people feel when they are alone that they have no one, or that they are no one." Joe rocked silently to the tempo of the piano. His wife's notes held the quality of rain, steady and spread out in the air. He repeated:

"The path of your fear. Yes. And thank you so much for coming to see me today."

Feo drove steadfastly under diminished sails — her smallest jib, the mainsail shortened down in size by a single reef and the mizzen sail aft. I was not sure whether this amount of sail was too much or too little. The barometer held steady at 1015. The stove swung steady in its gimbals so I could safely boil water for coffee and instant soup. I wolfed down a pair of peanut butter and banana sandwiches, anxious to use the fruit before it spoiled.

I kept climbing up into the cockpit to peer into the dark for freighter lights, monitor the compass and adjust the control lines for the steering vane, which held us within a few degrees of our southwesterly course. In the shaft of my pocket flashlight I could watch the blade of the vane tilting to the wind. Whenever Feo strayed off course, the resulting shift in her angle to the wind would press the upright blade of the wind vane. This in turn pulled wires that rotated a skeg underwater. The pressure on the skeg fed back through a set of pulleys and ropes attached to the tiller, which brought Feo back on course.

Throughout the night I kept coming into the cockpit to make sure the tireless little figure was still in control and the wind direction had not changed. It was becoming obvious through the reliable care-giving of this device why single-handed ocean sailors tended to name their wind vanes after their mothers.

Each time I came out of the cabin, the steep waves angling out of the north hissed like an audience of cynics and the whistling wind edged up another fraction of a tone. Or else it was my imagination, listening for what it feared. I could not see the surface of the water to judge the squalls except for flashes of whitecaps that peaked sharply at the windward rail, then foamed away flat to disappear into the dark.

Feo would roll down on each wave and angle back sharply over the next peak, falling swiftly into the next gully and then start back, over and over. In dim overhead light the cabin interior moved like a rail car sliding sidelong down an undulating hill. The ching-ching of antique Tibetan chimes in one corner became so insistent I stuffed them under a bunk cushion so I could hear only the movement of the water and the wind through the shrouds — and await the sound of freighter engines. I imagined that I would be able to detect the approach of giant propellers circling just in time.

———————

I fell now into a state of feeling I had never experienced, the apprehension that I might never return, never see anyone again, never hear another voice. I had told myself over and over that I was capable of this passage, that it was not suicidal, not a death wish insinuating itself into my life from recent disappointments. But I had not spoken of this to anyone, believing that talk of failure invites a bad ending.

This was the precipice of my own making, the private fear I had never faced, which now stared out from blackness characterized only by alien sounds and motion. In a space that seemed interminably high and wide and deep I fought a vertiginous sense of free-fall and dislocation. Steeped in the noise of Feo's onward plunging, I struggled to follow the instructions in the Loran handbook and program the computer to pinpoint my location. I had not expected to tackle it while braced on the ice-chest between the quarter-berth and companionway ladder, but here I was, trying to make myself too busy to feel afraid.

A rising chorus of waves on steel swept around the hull. Strange poundings emanated from the fresh water tanks beneath the cabin floor, like someone trying to get out.

"Galong! Galong!"

The Loran was supposed to hook onto distant radio signals as its master and the master's slave, the book explained, one far to the northeast and one slightly southeast. The Loran would measure the time it took for signals to arrive and plot Feo's position. I would soon know where we were, how fast we were moving and how long it would take to get to the next waypoint along the route.

Sudden gusts drove Feo down to her rail, green water rushing along the scuppers. An occasional wave caught her amidships with a thunderous crack and rolled her down onto her side so the foaming green rose along the portholes. My anticipation stretched out and down into the motion and sound until my breath tied itself to her every movement. After a while, the feeling of the rollers became the sight of them, and I began to know from sudden moments of weightlessness that a big one was coming just before it arrived.

At 4 a.m., the Loran announced we were at Latitude 37 degrees 38.06 minutes, Longitude 123 Degrees 03 minutes. We were making six knots over the ground going almost exactly southwest. This position, 26 miles offshore, put us well outside the shoals of California and into the deep.

If that first night was perfect darkness, the next day broke as perfect isolation, grey and ominously dark across the water, flat and yet not perfectly so. The bow pulpit plunged toward the water and rose amid black delivery trucks that rushed beneath the bowsprit, where I braced myself to take down the jib as if Feo were amusing herself to dangle me into heavy traffic. I could perceive that I was on a huge sphere that curved off at the edges — open utter emptiness itself, the absence of anything to break the void, nothing here except Feo and me and these looming elements, the collected potential of the weather withholding its intentions and the grey, twisting ocean herself, moving, moving, moving... The horizon contracted within a choker of low clouds.

The sheer expanse of it!

I had slept for a couple of hours, jammed against the port wall of the pilot berth, and waked just after daylight, damp from spray that had penetrated the hatch during my forays into the cockpit and back. Smells of salt and diesel and spilled coffee hung in the air. I had expected to concentrate all day on the Loran, calculate our position by dead reckoning and study the celestial process of turning a sun shot into a coherent position. There would be no visible sun to shoot today. Besides, the Loran would have all the answers.

Despite my earlier efforts, the mainsail slides had jammed when I tried to reduce sail several hours before. I abandoned the effort in the dark in hopes the wind would subside. Now the wind tore the tops off the whitecaps in smoky wisps and whipped through my parka hood with faint mewing sounds, a "near gale" on the Beaufort Scale, or about 30 knots worth. In the last 12 hours, the barometer had not moved from 1015 millibars.

I tried to ignore the stunning length of the rhumb-line etched to Hawaii, some 2,200 miles to go. I kept telling myself I could sail another 100 yards in all but the very worst conditions. So I focused on individual tasks, one by one.

Scan the horizon; record the wind direction, the nature of the sky and the barometer.

Turn out running lights right away (one full night had run the batteries down almost to the bottom). Examine the cabins for porthole leaks. Keep checking the bilge.

Run the engine to recharge the batteries. Without them we are a sitting duck for freighters at night.

Be alert for change.

A foot of yellowish water sloshed deep in the hold below the water tanks where Feo's steel innards had always been bone dry.

Where in the world had it come from? She must be leaking, but how fast? Had we hit something while I slept? Where are the quick-fix epoxy and wood plugs?

Sinking, I see myself struggling to cut the dinghy free from its lashings. It is over the side and I am in it, quickly capsized and drowned in this wind.

The bilge pump in the forward head exhausted the water in fewer than 20 strokes, a burst of activity that put me in a deep sweat. I watched the black rubber bladder fill-and-empty, fill-and-empty, like an old lung ready to crack of age. I had not checked this bladder before leaving and there were no spares aboard.

Calm down. The port side has been heeled underwater for hours. The water has either come in around the anchor chain as seas break over the bow, or maybe leaked into the bilge as Feo put her port side under. Michel said to plug the bilge pump outflow with a wine cork when she heels to port.

I forgot. I have no cork, and can't reach the hole now anyway. Crouched in the head among Angelica's wallpaper nudes, I am embarrassed by my sudden sense of panic.

The flat grey sky, circling wagons on a dark plain, signaled no change from morning to midday to late afternoon. In search of the clanking sound somewhere aft, I found that the steering cable, which ran from the wheel in the cockpit back aft to the tiller, joined by a small tensioning device, was trying to work itself free. I sat and taped the fastenings together so they couldn't unwind. The mizzen sail astern was missing its reefing line, which I had forgotten to install before leaving. I stretched out to the end of the boom to thread a line through the edge of the sail. The boom swung out over the water, and I hung there for several minutes to catch my breath. The rest of Feo vanished from my field of vision as I stared down into our receding path, ivory carved into dark jade.

I am walking down a deserted path into the Buddhist sanctuary in Osaka. A stand of yellow daffodils, and silence except for the sound of gravel beneath my shoes. What was the nature of solitude but refined perception? At the temple an old man in an orange robe sold trinkets and for 100 extra Yen a written oracle, with a printed number — No. 38 — exactly my age. I carried it to the stone bench in a garden of leafless trees and with a sense of magic about to unfold read the words:

"Overtaken by darkness and getting lost on my way,

I found the moon shining bright on the field path."

Nearing the daffodils I had been thinking about getting lost, and wondered how one is found. The oracle said there would be light on the path.

The reverie came and went. I would not fall and if I did, I could not be left behind because my harness would save me. But just then as I stepped back down onto the deck, the harness dropped off my chest onto the deck with a loud "Clank!!"

Trembling broke out along my arms. All that time staring into my own wake, I had been attached to nothing at all.

———————

Down below, the cabin danced beneath me and each navigation tool worked its way to the floor. With the motion too violent for cooking, I boiled small amounts of water and mixed instant oatmeal sweetened with syrup. Feo's motion was spinning the propeller shaft and heating the transmission. The shaft brake would no longer hold it, so I jammed a long screwdriver alongside the shaft to keep it still. The engine idled roughly for 40 minutes or so, enough to recharge the batteries, but had overheated by the time I shut it down. Maybe the heat was just me, closed off in the cabin humidity. I made a cup of hot chocolate and reached for the good luck charm, which brought my friend's face into the cabin, prominent cheekbones and angular jaw to match, a bit of Audrey Hepburn. She had sent along several tapes, and when the first one clicked into the player, Bobby McFerrin's voice rose above the rhythm of the hull.

> *"Here's a little song I wrote...*
> *You might want to sing it note for note...*
> *Don't worry...*
> *Be happy..."*

B y late afternoon the wind was howling and salt mist rose from the waves like pale shrubbery, proof of the heaviest weather I had ever seen in my life. I still could not un-jam the slides to get the main sail down to its second reef-point, so with no other way to reduce sail I crawled forward to take the jib off. Fierce breaking combers came on like sections of a jet-black tunnel, cut loose and rolling downhill across our course to the southwest. The upwind cloud-line was sickly yellow-gray and swollen, bunched together as if hiding something inside. I didn't dare leave the mainsail up through the night no matter how frightened I was to turn Feo up into these seas.

What if the mainsail stuck and would not come down? Soaked with spray I crouched in the cockpit and planned each step.

Turn the wind vane upwind to swing Feo up into the wind.

Get forward fast. Double-clip to the shrouds and mast. Stay clipped in every second. Wait 'til the main flaps, hoist the pressure off, let the sail come down if it will.

You cannot quit.

The deck will be awash for much of this.

I stared upwind at the advancing seas, trying to see a stretch where the peaks flattened out, thought I saw one coming, *just now!*

Unhook the vane, turn the pendulum -

Hurry!

Feo is pivoting upwind, her bow rising sharply. I am through the cockpit and hooked into the lifeline. Get forward on your knees, hook to the shroud, unhook, stand up by the mast.

Hold on!

The sail is beginning to thunder and crack in the wind PA-POW! PAPOW! Get braced.

Get the winch handle on!

The boom is flailing beside me, I might be standing on a wild horse riding in the back of a truck careering down a mountain road.

Unhook the winch brake, quick!
Don't drop the handle!

The sail is still stuck. Winch it back up to take the pressure off the slides, goddamn if it won't come down. Feo can't drive further upwind as the oncoming seas pound her mercilessly.

I am a small boy crouched behind my father in the cockpit of Candida. He is at the tiller as the spinnaker, the huge-bellied sail they have set for the downwind leg of this race, begins to roll us down in a gust. The halyard is caught somewhere near the top of the mast and the sail will not come down as we are rounding the leeward buoy and turning across the wind. The sail is now dragging Candida further over at an angle and down into a deadly position. Dad is fighting to push the tiller up to the high side to turn Candida away from the wind, but he is losing the battle. She is being overpowered by the force of the sail, the rail is deep under and we are hanging on with a terrifying sense of the deck going vertical, the water almost directly below us and Dad swearing at Uncle John Streeter, his oldest friend and Candida's owner, who is tugging violently at something on the foredeck:

C'mon John...
get that...
fucking...
sail...
down...!

I knew we were in trouble then because he had never spoken the 'fucking' word before. Just then the spinnaker halyard broke with a thunder shot and the sail billowed out and down into the water, taking us out of that race for good.

C'mon, Feo, please.

———————

Suddenly the slides race part-way down, only to jam again. Feo rolls further upwind and the heavy mainsail thunders up along the mast, whipping back and forth. In a rush, the sail clatters down onto the boom and is blown fiercely to the downwind side. The boom slams back and forth against my stomach. I have to contain the sail but I am held too tight by the safety harness to reach it all.

Get aft quick, reset the vane! Feo is bucking and rolling angrily, a wild horse struggling to free herself from the irons I have put her in. Without the mainsail she is not driven, and without the jib she is not drawn.

The deck is a rotating seesaw, side-to-side and end-to-end. I crawl forward from the cockpit, dragging the jib and getting ready to clip it back on. Out on the bowsprit, seawater explodes off my yellow rain gear to make me gleam like a dandelion in the sun.

Nestled securely into the metal triangle, I begin to clip the jib hanks onto the forestay, taut spring-loaded clips that fight my cold fingers. As the jib pops open, a gust snatches the jib bag and drives it 30 yards downwind before it catches a wave top and sinks.

I hear his footsteps first on the stair, rising methodically, because I have been told to wait for him. I always wait for the sounds to begin. The treads come along the upstairs hallway, firm and steady, steadily closer and louder. By now I am crying and trembling, and before he even enters the room I am begging him in a disembodied voice that is mostly a wail, please Daddy don't do this, I'm sorry I didn't mean to do it, whatever it was, please don't do this now. I cannot face him or stand the meaning of his jacket coming off but I know the intimate sound of the black rub-

ber hose against his fingers, his large hands flexing it out straight and his voice the same cold low tone, "Turn around, take your pants down — and bend over against the bed," and that thin tubing with a skin of its own makes a tiny mewing sound in the air. It is a magic wand that makes fire alight. There is the shrill sound of a small voice screaming in the bedroom, it is coming from the place on the floor between the two beds, and small hands have seized the scalding place to keep the burn from spreading.

"You will have to learn to take your medicine," he said. "And when you are ready to behave, you may come downstairs." He seemed proud that he could strike three times and leave a single mark.

I was startled at the speed with which the yellow sail bag fell behind and pictured a man floating in that yellow spot, drowning. A low white hull came alongside the spot and a hunched figure hooked the bag aboard. The boat motored on back to the city. Someone identified the bag, called my father. The empty bag was the only remnant of my passage. No one would know what had happened or what I brought here in the tapes and journals, to sort out or leave behind, to find my way back.

I think I was about eight or nine when my older brother took me aside and said: Don't you get it? You're not supposed to cry. That's the point. He said this with a mix of sympathy and irritation. When you keep your mouth shut and keep the pain to yourself — don't make any noise at all — he will not do it to you again. Geoff had the same prominent forehead, shock of brown hair, and grey-blue eyes as my father, and a voice of authority that you were inclined to believe, and the small muscle in his jaw *started working overtime as he told me this. He must have been fourteen but he showed elements of a man's face even then.*

Settled into a steadier motion Feo charged on across these darkening roiled seas that rose and approached like giant sculptures, sudden ships and sails among rocks and promontories where there could be none. I watched them rise and fall, near and far, dark to light to light to dark. Thrown up of their own weight they collapsed and vanished into sprawls of froth. The passage of time evaporated with them. I do not know how long I sat and watched, if I watched and dreamed, or dreamed that I was watching, and only remembered as I woke what I had seen before I slept.

I must have been 10 before I could focus my will to take such white-hot sensation without a sound. Wind it up in a knot and focus it on him with the helpless withering hatred I learned to feel from it. I remember his eyes then, and they were frightened. My brother was right. My father never did raise the rubber switch against me again, though I must have violated some of his commandments many times — deliberate disobedience, disrespect, willful impudence. And he never spoke of it to me, either, not ever.

Arm-weary and scarcely able to move, I had napped only two hours in two days and would not be able to stay awake through the night. Feo would cover plenty of ground through a night of fierce wind. I tried to remember who told me to sail awake at night and sleep in daylight. *The freighters are more likely to see you then.*

I stumbled below, switched on the steaming light to illuminate the staysail, my white ghost on watch.

How foolish was my freighter-fear in this plain of water! Out here, the intersection of a cargo ship with a boat as small as Feo would be so hugely, mathematically improbable.

Above a 2,000-fathom spot known as Erben Tablemount, now about 450 miles from the city, I resumed the tape recording I had begun for my father. I wanted to pass along my new recipe for Sailing-Alone-to-Hawaii-Exploding-Tuna-Casserole in the event he ever wanted duplicate my cooking under these conditions.

Part I: Sometime in the middle of the night, acknowledge that you are cold and starving. Dig out a sack of just-add-water Spanish rice, which looks in dim light like bark chips mixed with little flecks of rust.

Boil water while the pot is trying to jump off the stove at you. Put in a tablespoon of margarine from the leaking grease-pot that is fouling your ice chest — the melting margarine that has begun to find its own level in the absence of ice to cool it.

With the pot of water and its surface grease at a full rolling boil, dump in the bag of rice/rust. Cover the pot until the assorted mystery chips have absorbed the fluid.

When that mix is nearly done, add a small can of niblet corn — the one with leafy Green Giant on the label. Stir thoroughly. Eat as much as you can stomach. Go back to sleep.

Part II: Leave the leftovers uncovered in the oven. Because the stove is swinging about 20 times per minute to the north and south as you go west, the greasy rice will settle into a luminous precipitate on the bottom of the pan.

Wait one day.

Still starving, remove the congealed concoction from the oven. Stifled by the rank smell of your own T-shirt, look into the pan.

"YEEEAAAGGHH!"

As the sound of your own horror dies away, be aware that you must not throw edible food overboard while sailing alone. It is too taxing to cook in heavy seas. Besides, you crave something *hot*, you need something with *bulk*.

Empty a can of tuna fish into this concoction, which resembles the moonscape of Mars. Pour a small can of tomato sauce onto the tuna, then spread several pieces of bright orange cheese onto the lunar surface.

Braced tight between the stove and the companionway stairs, you realize you have never actually lit this oven, newly installed for this passage.

Set the dish aside. Read the instructions. Try to ignite the pilot light. This apparently requires a person with one arm twice as long as the other and with a thumb capable of pressing at 1500 pounds per square inch on a button that is beyond reach. Ignition can only be accomplished with your free hand groping the bottom of the oven with a lighted match that must be held motionless for at least 10 seconds above a little hole you can't see.

After you have scorched several fingers, an unspeakable smell emanating from the stove will confirm that an unnamed new-stove chemical is being burned off in a toxic cloud that is dissipating slowly in the cabin. Most of it is probably collecting in your lungs.

Now put the casserole into the oven. When the primordial ooze on the bottom begins to bubble, it will be done.

Part III. Now for the crucial finishing touch. Presentation is everything.

To open an oven door on a boat heading west and rolling north-south, you must stop the gimballed stove from swinging back and forth. This creates a frictionless downhill stainless steel chute inside the oven so the piping hot glass casserole dish full to brim with melted cheese and boiling grease rockets toward your bare hands and face as you roll backwards with the boat. Fortunately, because the human mind can see disaster unfolding a nanosecond faster than disasters unfold, you know where the casserole is headed and exactly what to do:

SLAM THE FUCKING DOOR!

Now, bobsled casserole meets spring-loaded door at roughly the speed of sound. Resulting explosion as liquefied tuna and cheese and rice coats oven and solidifies into blackened saddle leather.

Prop yourself up. Express yourself in rapid-fire Anglo-Saxon monosyllables. Try to hold the hot door open with one hand and scrape as much saddle hide off the oven walls as you can get into the dish.

Now *that's* dinner.

It actually tasted very good. Developments in the last few days had whetted my appetite. I had a lot further to go than miles.

I kept waking to the sound of metallic impacts and the sensation of my body striking the port wall beside the berth. The faintly backlit Loran screen above my head reported speeds up to 15 knots.

In theory, a boat cannot go through the water faster than its hull shape will allow. A formula puts that limit at roughly one-and-a-half times the square root of the waterline length. So with a natural limit of about 10 knots — if Feo were really hitting 15 knots with just two small sails up — her hull had to be "planing" down the waves, thereby overcoming the theoretical resistance. I did not want to go on deck to experience the sensation in the dark. That much speed had to be some kind of Loran calculation error.

I listened to the intermittent crash on crash on crash that spread along her hull and talked to her.

You have been here before and know what to do. Just get us through this night.

She bucketed and rolled and wrestled her way along, and I fell in and out of fitful sleep.

My father sat on the kitchen floor whittling a small block of pine. He had the large hands of his father, a small man who distinguished himself in the British Army as a boxer unbeaten in his weight class. The shavings came off in perfect curls, each a replica of the last. The rectangle gave way to curves and straight lines became a twist of grain. Then he held it out to me. The wooden block had become a propeller.

"Drill a hole through that, Laddy, and put it on a nail and see what it does," he said. "You see why it pushes water when it spins?" He had been waiting for me to come downstairs and his voice was unusually gentle.

I came into the cockpit to face relentless grey seas stretched out, rough and riddled with the intermittent squalls that had driven Feo throughout the night. I squinted up at the rigging. I should have come on deck the first time I thought of it, hours ago. The halyard for the staysail had come loose from the deck, run partway up the mast and raveled itself around the main halyard. A clot of tangled lines halfway between lower and upper spreaders, about 25 feet above the deck, now disabled two of Feo's four sails. I stared at it for quite a while as I contemplated my phobia of heights.

This knot will not untie itself.

No one else is going to do it.

Maybe I could stand on tiptoe on the lower spreader. If I held onto the mast with one hand and stretched to my limit, I might hook something onto the tangle to pull it down. The thought of standing aloft in the rigging made me want to throw up.

Well, maybe I could cover the remaining 1,800 miles on two small sails, *very* slowly.

"Yeah, well, maybe that's what you're so afraid of, but that's what you're going to have to do."

My own voice. I had been talking aloud the whole time I had been staring up, but heard myself clearly now for the first time.

❁

I would ignore the rigging problem as long as the wind persisted, and time collapsed into small adjustments. I fiddled with the wind vane to steer us further west. A quartering sea rolled up over the gunwale and into the cockpit, so I turned Feo back across the seas, giant dogsled without dogs, angling down one roving hill after another. I ate and napped.

Emily's note for today was a pile of individual letters, one scrawled on top of another until the scramble became undecipherable. Underneath in parentheses she had translated: I love you.

Once after I went into her cabin to shut off the small dome light and kiss her good-night. Her voice followed me back into the main cabin.

"Dad?

"Yes."

"I love you so-o-o-o much."

"I love you so much, Em. I loved you so much before you knew who I was."

"I loved you so much before I knew who I was," she said. "Good-night."

I had not been able to explain to her why I had to leave for several months, except to say that this was something I felt I had to do. I wished I could have said that things were coming together to make more sense of my life, and hers. But I didn't know that with any certainty, and saying it would have been the triumph of hope over experience. On a huge art pad I began a day-by-day illustrated diary to send her. Dad, the Stick Man, said good-bye to Pier 39, dodged the blunt pair of shark-headed freighters named Exxon and Toyota. The four points of the compass and a long arrow directed the red dot from a blob called California southwest toward some apparent insects in the distance.

Hawaii.

I could see her bright blue eyes, almond-shaped like her mother's, brightening at these drawings, so much a child's.

B reaking seas along the windward deck forced jets of seawater under the main hatch. I cut a thin strip of polyurethane packing material to form a crude gasket — not watertight, but tight enough. From the sail locker came a length of cord to bind the hatch shut from inside. It made me feel trapped below, so I retied the knot until it released in one quick pull, like a ripcord.

The cabin table disappeared under celestial texts and tables for the sun and moon and stars. I could not be lost at sea, the books reassured me, if I could establish the sun's highest point at midday — the oldest and most basic celestial calculation. Local noon of the sun translates into an exact latitude, which provides a fix north or south of the equator and west of Greenwich, England. Any measured angle of a celestial body above the horizon will produce its own line of position on the chart. If my sextant shot was accurate, I had to be somewhere on that line.

The engine ran for 20 minutes, its cover suddenly too hot to touch. I stared into the compartment for the source of smoke that mixed with cabin humidity into something like city bus exhaust. Beneath me from the water tanks came that odd honking sound again.

The noise an approaching freighter makes at night.

The Loran said we were now as far south as San Luis Obisbo and due south of Vancouver Island. We seemed to be descending from San Francisco on a charted flight of stairs southwest along the rhumb line. Feo and I were now disconnected from land and suspended from the heavens.

❀

By the next afternoon I had devised a way to go up into the rigging on a heavy rope into which I had tied a loop every few feet. My plan was to hoist one end up the mast and fasten the other to the deck.

With my harness clipped into one of the shrouds, I stepped up into the first loop like a short man mounting a tall stirrup. Just then a steep wave caught Feo sideways and the motion slung me around the mast like a rock on the end of a string. My right leg slammed into the main winch, which bit a small chunk out of my ankle. As the line recoiled again with me spinning on the foot of it, I grabbed the mast and shinnied back down onto the deck.

The seas are still too rough.

I slouched under the mast, feet braced in the lifelines, depressed not to have gained the first spreader. Wouldn't any rope suspended from a 50-foot mast— particularly with a man on the end of it — act like a whip? How stupid could I get? The bow wave sizzled past. The light grew tinny. There was no sun behind the metal. The source of light was everywhere, nowhere. The white and gold watch my wife had given me on our last anniversary had stopped. No amount of rewinding would restart it.

*W*e fought like cats and dogs in that rented Valley flatland house. I could picture myself standing over her as she sat on the couch. I was yelling something and she was giving me a shattered look, with big tears in her eyes. Another night of angry words were punctuated by threats that she would return east to her family. She repeated it again as I was in the shower and she began to wrestle her suitcase toward the door. Then somehow we were storming out together in pale dawn light toward Lake Tahoe, the magic elopement that was supposed to fix everything. A Philadelphia Jew and a New England Wasp the youngest of three with the youngest of three, two would-be writers — it had a certain symmetry on its face. She was slow to reveal herself and I could not hold my tongue nor keep the edge off it. Opposites attract. A pair of natural magnets? There was nowhere I could go in words she could not follow and maybe what we liked about each other's volatility was that we both had it, gift of our respective fathers. We rejected the first mouthwash-blue wedding chapel we came to in Lake Tahoe.

"I don't want to get married in a bottle of Lavoris," she said, which made us both laugh. We plunged up over the mountain ridge and down into the next valley to the Justice of the Peace in Minden. I smoked a joint as I drove and drank warm champagne from the bottle all the way from the car to the City Hall. A basement lectern served as the altar. We were both emboldened by romantic impulse — so I told myself — as I ignored the still, small voice that said, "this is not the right thing to do, this is not what you want." I wept when the final words pronounced us man and wife, feeling far detached from the meaning of my own tears. The official witness, whoever she was, thought them joy.

I knew this marriage would begin to fall apart as soon as I pressed on it with all my weight. Immediately but secretly I thought about divorce, but dared not say it aloud until she said it first. I said I didn't want to cause pain — or experience more of it, either — but I thought I was more afraid to be alone than anything. For a time I was consoled by her father's mantra from his own marriage, which he liked to repeat: "Conflict brings a couple closer." As a steady gin drinker with a wicked temper, he might say that.

The Valley wind swept over the small house and I heard the rattle of the windows like something blowing through me, a voice that kept saying that I was wrong and we were wrong and should end it. Prolonging doubt and conflict where there wanted to be certainty and peace only increased the pain. Wounds added to wounds.

I did not know what meaning to put on things as they were. I believed I could make things as I wished them to be. We bought a house in an old neighborhood, stripped wallpaper and refurbished kitchen countertops. I cleared backyard rubble, built a brick patio like the field stone terrace my father laid in Massachusetts three decades before, and set into Valley peat soil a variety of plants alien to my boyhood — peach and fig, Indian

71

Paintbrush, impatiens and pachysandra. Biology did not wait for serenity. Emily arrived one hot August morning as an explosion to my heart that transcended spoken word. Her small bright face soon bore witness to my own childhood shadows. Her father worked long hours, drank hard every night and disappeared into weekend tennis games. He provoked fights and flew into rages. Her mother and father fell into long bitter silences and went separately for days at a time. This child would be carved into separate refuges if no one saved her from it. I buried myself in the news of the Valley city, aware of something wrong at the core but unwilling or unable to face it. I did not listen in those early months, (which grew into years), to the lone voice within that knew — if only I had been able to listen. So after almost eight years we finally separated, and I came at last into Feo.

Several times recently in the public showers at the Pier I had left behind the watch she had given me, only to find it each time I went back for it.

"You just need to take time off," said a friend, making a joke of my carelessness with the watch. We were walking along the Pier at the water's edge. "You know, getting to the point of leaving can be as difficult as the journey itself."

T he wind dropped off to about 15 knots the next morning, a breeze that was brisk but now seemed docile. The tangled knot still hung in the shrouds, waiting.

I had seen boat-yard riggers clamber up between the heavy stays that converge where the spreaders meet the mast. One particularly agile friend, who had worked the high yards of a square-rigged ship for years, could shinny up hand-over-hand and then hook his feet and brace his shins against the wire to work with both hands free. I would have to get myself all the way onto the cross-tree and buckle myself to the mast.

I kept picturing it and getting ready to make a move. Then suddenly in one instant I found myself clinging by fingers and feet to the lower stays, the spreader suddenly under both arms, my knee upon it. The mast was cool and solid against my face, the spreader under foot. Intoxicated at this height, with Feo transmitting a Pacific cadence through the mast, I could see the curvature of the earth and myself on top of it.

I clipped my harness around the mast and drew myself up on tiptoe. Feo held me in the crook of her spars as I leaned out on one foot, hand aloft. Nothing in the world to see for a moment except that tangled knot and my fingers reaching for it, drawing closer.

I am no victim. This knot is mine.

From a distance I seemed to be watching the lone yellow figure partway up the mast, the deck below a yellow wink against the black ocean, trailing a frothy bridal train. Amid the thrumming of the rigging he sat embracing the mast and embraced by it, savoring triumph over an old enemy.

The bowsprit led on, vibrant arrow to the southwest.

All sails full, Feo emerged from under a roof of clouds stretching back toward the continent and churned along at six knots or better, her bilge dry. Four Loran positions over a day-and-a-half showed our course running just above southwest, 530 miles from the Farallons and slowing down. I reheated the remains of the exploding casserole, sat with earphones on and *La Boheme* in the cassette, and watched the dark bird that had been following Feo now for two days.

How did it manage to endure such distances? Did it see in this red steel body and fabric wings a hybrid relative, part fish and part bird? Did it ever think about solitude? Puccini's arias and the water and the bird, arcs and melodies and ellipses, danced through my thoughts like shadow puppets. Feo's motion was the ocean, was my motion, was my emotion. Sky and endless water were as much me as I was among them. I fell asleep in the cockpit and woke in the dark, enveloped in rhythmic sea sounds, just awake enough to climb below, flip on the running lights, and fall back to sleep.

A high-pitched "beep-beep-beep!" above my head jerked me awake again as Feo pitched along in the black. The screen of the Loran had gone around the words:

"Down, please off."

Conscious of my heart beating aloud, I flipped the switch for the battery indicator. The needle did not move.

The house batteries are dead. Automatic navigation is dead. Running lights atop the mast are out.

Feo can't be seen.

In a few moments I started the engine, almost certain it would fail.

Ten minutes later, with a small charge back in the batteries and the Loran back on, the engine died again. Restarted, it ran for a few minutes and died again. I didn't dare restart it without

---

finding the source of smoke so evident in the blade of the flashlight. It was nearly midnight.

By noon the next day, squeezing myself into the engine compartment had me drenched with sweat, bracing against the roll and yaw of Feo running downwind. Tools were strewn across the cabin floor. I was less than an amateur engine mechanic and knew it.

Checking for air in the fuel lines, I broke a crucial plug, which bled diesel into the bilge. It took several hours with a hacksaw and file to fashion a new plug from an old bolt, cut and honed to fit. All the incoming water and fuel lines seemed to work. The engine finally restarted and I peered over the side to check for cooling water outflow.

None.

So, salt water coming into the cooling system was not passing through it. The engine had overheated, perhaps internally damaged. Holding the flashlight at an odd angle I could see a leak low down between the seawater pump and engine block. So *that's* how water was getting down into the bilge!

The Loran flashed a warning that it had locked onto an unreliable signal, probably too far from the continent. Power for the Loran would soon be gone anyway.

We would be two weeks with no lights, invisible to anything that approached in the dark. I didn't yet know how to locate myself.

Celestial is your fail-safe.

I *said to Brody, I don't know how it's going to come out.*
There's a weight that comes with trying to get to a different place.
The challenge is to be honest about what's going on. I hope I'm not
bullshitting myself.

You think you are bullshitting yourself? he said.

I don't think so. An argument can rise so quickly that I
lose track of what's true. Part of me now is in terror of losing my
grip. The storm is here and I am hanging on and I'm going to get
through this. I'm not here by accident. In the worst times, I know
I am a survivor.

The bird was back, solitary speck with a white crown over
his beak, hovering close, watching. I had no reference book to
tell me his species or what he might be doing. As I crouched in
the stern to rig the taffrail log that would measure our distance
covered, I called to the bird, just across a short stretch of water
astern where he floated, unblinking.

"What do you think?"

The taffrail log, an old device for measuring distance traveled by a sailboat, had a metal spinner that trailed overboard
at the end of a line. This line turned gears of a small measuring gauge on board. I should have been using it from the moment we left the Golden gate to calculate our distance over the
ground, independent of the Loran.

We had averaged about four knots for 18 hours since the
last Loran fix early Tuesday, Greenwich time.

We needed to know exactly how much ground we covered
along the course.

What about daylight savings time?
What?

Spring forward, Fall back.

Which?

Was it nine hours from Greenwich to here, or eight in mid-summer? Or was it ten?

The book said: The only time that matters is Greenwich-based, the universal clock for navigators. The earth is revolving west to east. The sun takes 24 hours to circle the globe, moving west at 15 degrees an hour. Each 15 degrees marks another time zone, one hour further from Greenwich. This stretch of ocean from 127 to 147 degrees West Longitude, had to be nine hours later than Greenwich.

Ah. Daylight savings is irrelevant here.

The moment the sun stops rising overhead and starts back down will mark local noon — the instant of meridian passage.

The angle of a celestial body above the horizon does not lie.

You've never done this. Wait 'til you get close to shore.

The heavens will always tell you where you are.

The sun travels at 900 miles an hour. A minute's error is a 15-mile error in position. Four seconds a mile.

One voice in my head demanded to know all the right answers right now. Another voice, just as authoritative, cast doubt.

You've never done this before, you don't know what you are doing.

I wondered whose voices they were, where they came from? Maybe after a while I would begin to hear the voice I wanted to identify as my own.

The breeze had come up mild and steady from the north-west. Parallel rollers unfolded as somber dunes along a line west-south-west, infinitely grand reverberations of a planetary boulder, dropped eons ago. Topaz blue sparkled bright with intermittent whitecaps, impeccably rich jewel of unbounded water. The vane cocked slightly to shift Feo south. I stood on the aft hatch, my back against the mizzen, Feo's rigging taut and gleaming and purposeful against the sky, and watched her bowsprit cleave across this darkly gorgeous, ageless plain.

In 1699, Sir Isaac Newton discovered a way to hold a mirror up to the sun to reflect its image onto another glass, through which the observer would simultaneously view the horizon. The angle of the mirror reflected the sun's angle above the horizon.

The modern sextant that evolved from Newton's concept remains a mysterious object to most people because few have ever had any occasion to use one. A small mirror on a swing arm is hung on a frame shaped like a wedge of pie. Holes in the frame permit you to hold the apparatus so that the edge of the pie slice faces you. Through an eye-piece along one side you sight the horizon on a filtered glass, onto which the mirror casts the sun's image.

The swing arm has teeth and a gear and a measuring dial that move it in precise increments along an arc. As the sextant is held in the left hand, the right hand is free to turn a dial to capture the sun's height in degrees, minutes and seconds. The measured angle and its exact moment of occurrence are the heart of the celestial calculation — "the sight."

In a rare moment now the sun fell round and perfect yellow towards a cloudless horizon. The full moon rose silk and silver pale in the blue afternoon. There the two hung, west and southeast, a pair of perfect targets in the clear.

This was the prize opportunity that Celestial Sam had spoken of — a shot at two bodies, high enough above the horizon to escape the distortion of light being bent around the earth's curve. Two lines of position, one solar and one lunar, would provide a reliable fix.

Holding the sextant at the ready, I braced myself against the main hatch, like a hunter whose awareness has been attracted skyward by the sound of distant birds, the right moment for shooting still to come.

I understood the theory this way: All celestial bodies are on the same imaginary sphere around the earth, like a planetarium ceiling. Picture the line from the center of the sun to the center of the earth. The line goes through the ocean on a particular spot. How far you are from that spot, and in which direction, can be calculated from the sight-reduction tables.

That spot is also the center of a circle that you must be on somewhere. On the plotting sheet you draw a fragment of that circle, so small it appears as a straight line. This is your "line of position." Draw another line based on a sight of the moon. You are wherever those two lines cross. This is your "fix."

The sextant is supposed to be handled like fine china and painstakingly maintained. Mine was a lightweight, plastic model, a gift from my father that he had sent along with the taffrail log and a chart-plotting device. "The Director" could lead anyone out of confusion once they got into it, he said.

This sextant was as accurate as its heavy bronze ancestors common to the Navy, he had said, but would be easier for a beginner to manage on a small boat.

Whatever precision the instrument holds, error is assumed on any boat in motion. The sextant must be vertical when the measurement is taken, which can be very challenging even in a moderate seas. Fearful I might knock the instrument out of whack, I babied it like an explosive that might go off in my hands.

Nothing here now but the ocean and sky surrounding two suspended medallions — no sound or sense of flight or movement beyond Feo's steady rhythm to the southwest, the wash, re-wash, re-wash of her bow wave, graceful and deliberate. In that calm and steady motion, the wind now dying off by degrees, I brought the sun into the small mirror. Squinting through the view-finder, I marveled at the impeccable round orb that swung like a shiny clock pendulum through the bottom of the arc to the other side. I moved my hand the other way.

The orb came back through the bottom of the arc again, a hair above the horizon line, and approached that razor's edge as I dialed the sextant mirror down, and up, and down again as the hull rose and fell. I waited to be on top of the wave for the orb to touch. Almost...

Now!

The orb grazed the line.

Time: 23 hours, 43 minutes and 47 seconds. The sextant angle read 52 degrees, 56 seconds.

Two minutes and two seconds later, I shot the moon's angle: 28 degrees, 28.8 minutes.

These numbers begin a computational process — some call it telephone-book arithmetic — to produce lines of position on the chart. In primitive times, navigators had to make brutal calculations of spherical trigonometry to fix a vessel's distance from the sun's ground position. The work was so laborious that tables were devised for all the days, times and angles of the sun, moon and stars. The simple time and angle now would locate our ground position.

The angles of the sun and moon must be adjusted for the height of the navigator's eye above the water and refraction of light in the atmosphere. The moon needs a few other adjustments because it is so close to the earth and moving so fast across the sky.

Taken from two different tables, the numbers entered a workbook of narrow columns. Addition and subtraction of hours and minutes and seconds, angles and degrees and tenths of degrees, some negative and some positive, depending on additional factors found on some other page, proved a sinkhole of despair for anyone like me who had never actually managed to balance a checkbook.

You assume that you know roughly where you are — your "dead reckoning" — and plot your ground position from there. But plotting sheets for ocean navigation take on an eerie reality. A circle quartered by cross-hairs, one longitude and one latitude, is divided into 360 degrees of the compass. Five latitude lines are provided and you must draw longitude lines according to scale for your part of the world. The distance between longitude lines, which converge as they run from the equator to either pole, must be adjusted to reflect your distance from the equator.

After two hours of computing and re-computing small sums and differences, measuring degrees and miles out onto the worksheet (every minute of latitude is a mile) and drawing a series of lines, I finally reduced the angles of the sun and moon to two short pencil lines on the chart.

The lines crossed!

Intersection of sun and moon declared me to be at 30 degrees, 40 minutes North Latitude, 134 degrees, 39 minutes West Longitude — 650 miles southwest of San Francisco, about 95 miles south of my rhumb-line course.

I penciled the fix firmly onto the chart in a spot about halfway between Erben and McKinley Seamounts. The line of Loran fixes over the previous few days had been pointing toward this area, which gave my fix real authority.

Overjoyed with the apparent clarity of the answer, I did not consider what it meant now to be 55 miles northeast of where I had thought I was.

Did it matter, really, way out here?

I tidied up the navigation books and climbed out in the cockpit with my last bowl of Exploding Casserole, to watch this peaceful night come on.

Grey and black and purple robes hunched along the horizon line to the west. Behind them the sun burned holes to touch off a fire that spread and liquefied, running east on languorous swells, blocked by the sudden rise of a roller, which emptied itself with a racing flood of brilliant white. The lava flashed and stabbed along these rollers in parallel flight, detoured at odd angles by crossing waves, then set itself loose again in long, instantaneous troughs of sheen. More distant dark rollers rose and fell, filling with light and emptying again, humpback whales lit by the glow. The brilliant liquid broke into smaller and smaller pieces as it came closer until it dissolved close at hand on tiny wavelets near the hull.

High to the southeast now the moon eluded dark evening clouds and cast a silver path to converge with the sun's brilliant stream. Feo found herself intersected by a path of gold from the west and one made of silver from the southeast.

"Here you are," proclaimed the sun and moon together. "Look! You are here."

*M*y father took me out for a ride one Saturday morning in his black '59 Buick, the one the company gave him to drive. I was still small for the front seat and the wind blowing in through the windows smelled of autumn leaves. It soon became clear we were not driving anywhere in particular.

"So, Laddy. What's the worst word you know?" he asked, his voice unusually gentle. He almost never called me Laddy. He was looking straight ahead at the road.

My face flamed. Surely he didn't want me to say that word.

"Bastard?" I suggested.

"Really?" he said. "I thought perhaps you might know the word "fuck" by now."

"Yeah, well," I said, hoping to obscure the thing altogether.

"Do you know what it means?" he said.

I mumbled something about not being really sure. Maybe some kid at school had said it, I wasn't sure if I had heard it correctly. Nobody seemed to know much about it. No, I didn't know.

An overwhelming silence had invaded the car, in which he said:

"It is something sacred between men and women. It's not a dirty word — not when it means love-making between a man and a woman who love each other. It's something God gave to man and it's not something we take lightly. Not ever."

I was not sure why he mentioned God now since we did not go to church. He had gotten sick of it from early school and his mother's preaching, my brother told me. The God word was never supposed to be spoken casually, though, and this other word was way out of bounds. I know if I were to let it slip I would get sent upstairs for "a switching," as my mother liked to call it.

"If you really loved a woman, you wouldn't make love with her unless you were married to her, do you understand? Love-making that has nothing to do with love is just sex. Then it's wrong and people get hurt. Do you understand what I mean?"

"Yes," I said, awash in a vague notion akin to delirium, if I had known what delirium was then. Wouldn't this ride ever end? We seemed to be driving around in circles and so were my thoughts.

❀

I was trying to explain to Brody, remembering the Buick: love and sex and marriage were supposed to converge in a perfect union. That was the official birds-and-bees conversation. The message was: sex without marriage is without love and therefore wrong.

So then when I lost my virginity in the back of a speedboat on Lake Winnipesaukee, the end of a booze-cruise a deux, and caught gonorrhea from a very pretty and wealthy girl of good family you would never have suspected, I thought maybe my father had been onto something. The punishment fit the crime.

You decided it was wrong? Brody asked.

I don't know. I thought I was in love with her, and I had waited for a few months before being ready to do it with her. The truth is she knew a lot more than I did and sort of decided for me, in the way it happened. Anyway, I was still hung up on that North Carolina girl who I had really wanted to marry when I was 17. And later, making love in graduate school before I got officially engaged, the pleasure of it tipped me into a terrifyingly huge space that left me with a sense of sadness and loss I couldn't explain. I guess I didn't want that feeling to happen, not then.

You didn't want to get involved that way?

I didn't want it to be casual. It was supposed to be—

When you had made this commitment?

When I actually had this commitment, part of the commitment. One sanctified the other. I didn't want to go to that place under casual conditions. I suppose I wanted it to be perfect.

Perhaps this connects with your father saying that this is what is supposed to be.

I think so, absolutely.

The message was that sex outside of marriage was going to make you feel guilty, which is interesting, said Brody. When you first started today you were talking about feeling unsuccessful in your marriage.

The sails slatted and banged. Feo rose and fell in a prairie of open water, undulations serene and mysterious for the distances they traveled, origins unknowable, perhaps an Asian typhoon somewhere. How much of my life had I struggled to free myself from something? What was it? Would I ever know what it was?

Feo turned to face the moon, a faint wind coming from astern that was barely enough to feel on my wet finger held aloft. The sails hung idle. The masthead telltale, that jaunty little triangle of plastic on a swivel, was turning full circle in search of what little wind there might be. Some words emerged in my journal:

What there is
There is in me
If only I
could only see.

The batteries drained down to almost nothing and the Loran finally quit. Loran trying to hook onto land-based stations would be useless this far offshore even if the power had not failed. One flashlight bulb after another expired until I had only one small one left, wrapped in a plastic sandwich bag to protect it from moisture. I nurtured it like a pet bird that might be killed in a careless moment.

The barometer held steady at 1020 for four days, and I spent two afternoons trying to reach the leak in the engine, beginning with a mysterious aluminum bulb tucked down behind the engine. I pored through the Yanmar engine manual and diagrams and confirmed the worst.

Whatever was leaking lay on the underside of the engine. A flap of rubber protruded into a puddle of rust water at the limit of the flashlight's little glare. Maybe a gasket blown. I replaced several zinc plugs designed to protect the diesel against corrosion. The one nearest the water pump was almost entirely decayed. Maybe something vital in the pump had dissolved, victim of salt water.

Even if I can get to the problem — if I can figure it out — I probably will not be able to fix it.

"You don't begin to know enough." My father's words came into the cabin, his grim face alongside in judgment.

Several toolboxes were wedged beneath the cabin table, stray parts spread around me on the aft cabin floor, a rag stuffed into the engine where the bulb had been. Feo felt disemboweled, along with my confidence.

I struggled to stay awake at night under a glittering panoply so vast and magnetic that it seemed to draw conscious thought into the atmosphere. I had never been a student of astronomy but was now suddenly aware how disconnected from the universe I felt.

The bright, yellowish-white point was Jupiter. The Big Dipper I knew. The two stars at the end of the bowl point to Polaris, the North Star.

In the opposite direction was Leo, with Regulus the bright star at the end of the sickle. Follow the curve of the Big Dipper's handle the thickness of three fists held aloft, to Arcturus.

Yes, I see.

Where is the Great Square of Pegasus, and Cassiopeia?

After some time I was no longer quite awake, yet not asleep and not dreaming and not here, but elevated among pinpoints of light, spread out and unconscious of the dark. Time was nothing.

An entranced feeling overcame me, looking up from the ocean into the universe at 31 North Latitude, basking in star patterns I had never seen. Connections and distinctions existed through human consciousness. They defined me as I defined them.

We make our own place in the infinitude in the manner of our being and nothing can take that away. Each of us occupies a spot entirely our own.

Abeam to starboard rose an endless mountainside, like distant house lights across a lake, pinholes in a dark curtain. Polaris hung within a degree or so of the northern celestial pole. The book assured me that with a few simple calculations I could determine our latitude from its angle, but when I captured Polaris in the mirror, I lost the horizon, and when I found the horizon again I lost Polaris. In the tiny luminous square of glass, the mirror and the night sky became the same to my untutored eye, so I finally gave up in frustration, believing I might have caught the star once, at about 31 degrees.

Combing stars at the horizon with the binoculars all around, I searched for any point of light moving left or right or approaching, any sign of a ship advancing along the bottom of that celestial sphere. Some stars pretended to be orange or red for a moment, or maybe something in my eye or mind changed the colors, which returned to white.

I gave up the search and went below for a few hours. I woke to make neatness my obsession. If everything were not in its place, something might be wrong with me, or I would be caught unprepared for the emergency when it came.

⚛

The lone brown seabird that had been following me day to day now sat about thirty yards away, rising and falling with the waves. I did not assign it a gender but felt that it might be the embodied spirit of someone from somewhere, sometime. I had been alone now for more than a week, the longest solitude of my life. Nothing suggesting another human had even appeared on the horizon. Listening to an aria from the first act of *La Boheme* by Italian tenor Carlos Bergonzi, I imagined that this bird was listening to the music, its head cocked alertly toward the notes across the water. They recalled Bergonzi's last recital in San Francisco, when one of his extended tones rose straight up in the air above his face, spread out and vaporized to envelope the audience like atmosphere itself. The perfect note.

In the calm that follows, the sails slat and the wind tell-tale at the top of the mast rotates to no purpose. The wheel lies idle. The steering vane is useless. I drop the sails because I cannot endure their sound, only to hoist them again minutes later on the hint of breeze because I cannot bear to be still. Flotsam appears alongside, stops with us and floats where we are, mocking the idea of forward passage. Feo seems to float past the same debris that has just floated past her.

The brown bird is up to glide a whisper's breath from the wave tops. Millennia of evolution are collected in its perfectly arched wings. It is searching for something.

The windless water rolls Feo side to side and redirects her despite any effort to steer. The Pacific high pressure system has imposed its ceiling of calm.

The shiny lure I have been towing overboard for the last two days shows no signs of attracting prey. I replace it with a clump of green-eyed plastic hair, with a wicked-looking hook embedded, legacy of Michel's trolling.

On the Voice of America, the Giants have beaten the Astros. There is talk of a pennant shot.

Sitting in the cockpit in this aimlessness, eating a sandwich and reading, I look up for no particular reason.

Is that a wave? A sail?

I spot a moving thing in the distance, coming fast. Is that a freighter steaming this way?

The bearing compass indicates the thing is approaching from 112 degrees. If this number does not change — from the size and shape I believe the thing must be a freighter — we're on a collision course.

Through the binoculars I can make out the arc of its bow wave. The bearing compass reads 102, but Feo's rolling side to side must be worth 10 degrees either way, so I am not sure what to think.

The chances of collision are too remote to take seriously.

By now the freighter has cut the distance by a third and I can see her bow wave clearly on both sides of her immense prow. The bearing compass says 112 again.

Coming at me.

"Feo to unidentified freighter in the vicinity, over." My radio transmission light flickers on and off as I speak.

"Freighter in vicinity, freighter in vicinity," I repeat. "Do you read me? Come in, please."

No response. They are supposed to answer you, even out here.

Is there enough power left in the batteries to transmit even a mile? The water pump is still in pieces, the breeze too faint to be felt. Feo has too little headway to respond to the wheel. We are just drifting.

Dead in the water.

I climb back up into the cockpit to recheck the freighter's bearing — 110 degrees.

Thirty seconds later, 113 degrees.

I can see the freighter's bow clearly, black vertical knife blade carving the water.

Will the diesel run with the water pump exposed? It is now obvious to me that the bilge has been collecting salt water leaking out of the cooling system.

Better burn up the engine getting out of the way than to be run down.

The bearing compass says 110–115 degrees, one swell to the next. The freighter is voraciously devouring rollers, two-by-two, on our converging path. My flare gun is loaded and ready in the cockpit.

I dive below to the engine, drain off some fuel, flip the power switch, and jump back into the main cabin to hit the starter button.

Start!

The engine catches.

The screwdriver! The propeller shaft is still pinned to keep it from spinning!

I tear up the floor hatch and reach down to yank the screwdriver free.

The dark shape, white above black, tiny stern tower eyes above the advancing snout, is closing, closing. I have Feo turning.

A voice crackles up from the radio below.

"This is the Bohini. What do you want?"

His bow will cross us by barely two hundred yards to the north.

I drop below to shut down the engine and grab the radio to reply:

"En route Hilo, single-handed. Can you give me our position?"

Smoke and the smell of hot metal infuse the cabin.

"Just a moment."

The Bohini is now framed through one porthole, rows of grey containers stacked beneath yellow cranes. A deep throbbing stimulates Feo's floorboards.

"Thirty degrees, thirty-nine minutes North Latitude. One hundred thirty-five degrees, fifteen point zero seven minutes West "Lon-git-tood." He pronounces the hard G and repeats:

"One-three-five degrees, One five point zero seven minutes West Lon-Git-Tood. Over."

"Thank you, over.."

"Who...are...you?"

"Feo, out of San Francisco. Where are you headed? Over."

Radio crackle breaks his reply into fragments. "Vn... coo..... vr."

"One other thing, Captain..."

"Yes."

"Did you see me on your radar?"

He does not answer. I see no signs of life on Bohini's deck as she crosses our bow just a hundred yards ahead. In less than 10 minutes she is as small as when I first saw her. In another 5 minutes, she is invisible.

So the sailor was right. They can get over the horizon in about 15 minutes and if you are not looking you will not know until they are on top of you.

The passing of the Bohini marked the beginning of the great dead spot, days of drifting, rolling frustration, barely 60 miles in 30 hours, in which the movement of air slowed and crawled about and stopped.

Breathless heat drove me out of the cabin and around the deck. I become hostage to small moving triangles of pale shade as Feo shifted on this slow motion screen of reflected grey sky.

She rolled up one side of a smooth wave and down the other.

Up one side, pause at the top.

Down the side, pause at the bottom.

Roll.

Up the side, pause. Down one side.

Roll.

The swells were no longer crossing right to left but left to right. She aimed northeast. It did not help to put the wheel hard over because there would be no wind. Stuck in this boundless pond, we were all slow motion and deck sounds. No faint wake declaring slow passage. The motion of the hull forced the boom across the cockpit and back, lines dragged across metal, metal across metal, scrapes and rattles in every pulley.

The mainsail emptied,

swish-crack

swish,

swish-crack

The sound repeated like a child with a toy bull-whip, preoccupied with duplicating noise.

I am forced in circles by zephyrs too faint to be felt, we circle debris as it circles us, plastic soap bottles, styro-foam fragments, bits of wood, mysterious angular objects that poke above the surface in the distance. There is no telling how large they are or how deep they go, whatever they are.

The wind-vane stood disconnected, useless, metal everywhere hot to touch, flecks of varnish peeling off the wheel, tattered by sunlight.

I said to Brody, let me line things up like this. I have uncertainty and conflicts about how I'm going through my life. I always have. I separate from my unhappy marriage and suddenly uncover the part of me that always wanted to live on a boat. Immediately upon buying the boat I am terrified of having bought her and possessing her. The moment I look at her as my own I can see all the inadequacies and faults I didn't see when she was still a fantasy. This reminds me how life is truly solitary. Your big choices are all ones you must make on your own. I say, "Steady, the fear comes with the territory. Stay with it and see what happens."

And what happens? Brody asked.

The boat makes me very happy. It feels right. You were right, to tell me to keep listening to that voice. I get closer to going out there alone, pushing myself through the risk, the fear. You know what I notice?

What do you notice? he asked.

I took Feo's steering system apart to rebuild it, every cable and turnbuckle, so I can believe in it. It's all part of the same thing — my life up in the air, trying to put it together so I believe in it. My life. No single part separated from any other — not you, the people I'm spending time with, people I'm trying to listen to, trying to rebuild the steering. You're all connected and things will turn out okay. In the good moments I believe that. But in the dark moments some other voice in my head is saying: You're wrong, you're crazy, you're full of shit, a fool, a phony, a dilettante. You're not going to make it.

T he sea is smooth imitation sky. The floating trash stays with me for hours. Overcast persists and I cannot see the sun for a sextant shot.

What if the Bohini had run us down? Would they have stopped? Who would ever report it?

I take the sails down to stop the incessant snap-and-bang and Feo behaves like a compass needle searching for a north pole that does not exist.

What if the wind never comes back? Do I have enough food and water? I scrub the stove and sink, sponge off the cabin floor, straighten the navigating books, and add another drawing to Emily's calendar. The Stick Man on Day 12 is sitting under an orange sun amid lifeless sails, his back to a dead engine, uttering to no one:

"Darn!"

I catch the sound of my own voice, snatches of alien phrases on the lifeless water. I keep seeing the Bohini, approaching and then passing at close quarters. How could two vessels intersect so perfectly in an expanse of four million square miles? My probability argument has dissolved. I am defenseless.

You have to watch. Maintain a good watch.

Unclear on Feo's meanderings amid these surface currents, I am unable to reduce a pair of afternoon sun shots taken through a thinning layer of cloud. I am not sure where to start the calculation if I do not know where I am to begin with. The two sun lines do not cross.

Bring the earlier line of position along the line of your course to the time of the second line.

I will be out here long enough to figure this out.

I awake with Feo lying westerly in flat seas on an endless undulating gymnasium floor. She has been turning in circles. How long could a boat with no engine remain trapped in this circle of calm?

"In every life expect some trouble, when you worry you make it double, don't worry... Be happy!"

The Bobby McFerrin tape is morning reveille. The sea and sky and silence are all grey except for an occasional pop-slat in the sail disturbed by a deep clunking of the rudder post underwater and squeaks in the block for the mizzen sheet. Sounds amid faint motion become the only reality: metal on metal, mizzen blocks clanking aft, reefing lines gently brushing the mainsail, gurgle outflow of the exhaust pipe at the waterline, burbling, gargling, gagging. Feo etches herself in sound.

I have the hint of a sore throat. Megavitamins pressed on me by a friend on departure had turned my urine green and scared me into thinking I had developed some deadly infection. I had quit taking them regularly because I didn't like to piss lime Kool-Aid overboard every morning.

The taffrail log hangs straight down off the stern, no hint of ripple on this water. It is grey all the way west where a thin line of last night's horizon still clings, coliseum roof trying to slide open. On Australian national radio, the Prime Minister has announced his country will not welcome the U.S. trying to relocate its air bases from the Philippines in the post-Marcos era.

Exhausted by all the noises, I keep the bow west for several hours, watching and waiting. The boom bangs back and forth. The compass needle crawls across "N." Feo drifts on around south and east. The sea is implacably smooth. A green glass orb probably used to float a fishing net stares up at me like a passing eye. I lash the main amidships and tie the rudder to the center-line. The bow will face whatever wind there is.

A puff of wind marks the water to the east, now the west, tantalizingly close abeam, but no effect. It comes closer.

Monitor your food intake, conserve.

My father has come downstairs in his white tie and tails. His top hat is cocked at a rakish angle, and with white scarf and gloves in hand he has a rakish grin to match that you could see for miles. My mother is close behind. Her floor-length claret taffeta gown, which she has had hand-made for the occasion, is singing with small sounds. They are about to compete in Boston's annual waltz evening, a kind of elevated amateur night with a few pros thrown in. My father believes they may win this time. They might be dressed for a 1940s movie, and whatever is wrong between them does not show. In a moment my father is out in the Buick, now honking impatiently. My mother is checking the stove to make sure no burners are on.

"Did anyone see me smoking? Would you please check all the ashtrays? I know I had a cigarette lit somewhere." Mrs. Davis from up the road is trying to shoo my mother out so we can start our game of gin-rummy. The house has the feeling of the pleasure they take together in these evenings.

The wind is now from the south, or Feo has swung, or both. I am trapped by a breeze that isn't there. I have been reading a murder novel in which an attorney is on trial for killing his lover. His wife is a shadowy suspect in a small community, riddled by deception and mistrust, an Updike novel gone bad.

From the cabin top I stare across the field of flat cloud, searching for movement. I have promised my editor at the Examiner that I will file a story on my solo crossing a week after I get there. Maybe he'll take a sidebar on ocean pollution. Multiplied by millions of square miles, the visible flotsam I see every day multiplied by four million square miles must be adding up.

The lone bird is arcing across Feo's trajectory several hundred yards to the south. Is it the same one? What does it perceive, black bump on this grey, a friend in spirit. Could it be spirit itself? It is asking me if I want to go for a swim.

I have no desire to join the food chain. When I was two-and-a-half years old on a family visit to British Columbia for my grandparents' 50th wedding anniversary, I pushed aside an empty barrel on a public wharf and fell through the hole it was meant to cover. At the time my father was still on crutches from a recent leg operation and he threw them aside to dive headlong through the opening, striking a piling with his shoulder on the way down. He dove repeatedly until he found a red sweater with me in it, and pulled me up into waiting hands before going into shock. I never developed a taste for swimming, even when he tried to cure me of that fear by throwing me in off the dock in Maine when I was five.

"Humans can all swim when they have to," he said. "That's how we learned as boys."

Getting in over my head had been my idea of a nightmare ever since, one sure way to make me panic.

T he cloud cover turned translucent to reveal the hot orb behind. Feo headed east. I would make the effort to turn her, but the wind would only shift and die again.

I had not eaten, caught up in this first novel of a writer just a year or two older than myself. I am dead in the water, too. What is the wind that does not blow in me? Afraid to start? Afraid to fail? Afraid to be judged for what I might reveal?

H eavy grey clouds are rolling in from the northwest the next afternoon when I catch the sun's peak at 82 degrees, 58 seconds. I had been sitting on the aft hatch, shooting the sun's angle every three minutes. Not even the Navy expects a celestial navigator to be reliable for the first 3,000 shots.

Down below into the cabin's humidity, I cannot make sense of the sun's latitude.

"The sun's declination for the estimated time of local noon is taken from the almanac and added to Z if the same name as declination, (north or south)," says the book.

Was the sun to the south?

According to my calculations, Feo is an impossible 150 miles northwest of where I think she must be. How, after hours of going nowhere, could we jump up so far to the north?

Open-faced and mute, the books and worksheets stare up in endless little numbers. The cabin rocks in humid indifference. I can't find the error.

Take a break. Make a cup of tea. Repeat the calculations.

Maybe the little compass magnets that correct for compass error have come loose from the deck.

Of course they have not.

My watch alarm signals that it is now Tuesday in Greenwich. I don't know exactly where I was on Monday.

Daylight savings? I return to the beige book of tables and recheck every number. Ha! I copied the wrong declination of the sun. The correct figure only brings the position south 15 miles. How many other errors can I *not* see?

Becalmed, drifting, making a few faint miles to the west. A total of 74 miles in the last 20 hours, the log claims.

My mind swarms. The variation in the earth's magnetic field here is 16 degrees east. I must be traveling south of west because the sun has been setting off the starboard bow. Since I have known where I was, what could be going wrong?

Maybe I never knew where I was.

Nothing has changed. Sit tight on this course southwest and see where you are tomorrow.

———————

The lawyer in the novel is caught up in love and desire, conspiracy and betrayal. Politicians are all liars and the liars are all politicians. He sensed the end of his marriage before anyone else could have suspected.

A torn sound rises into the sails, spreads out into sail whispers and clanking.

Do you want to reclaim it?

The question rises into the sound and silence of water all around and I follow it down a long hallway, between rooms of intimacies good and bad, her wit and a quick writer's mind that captures detail. She also learned as a small child to hide from a father who drank his three or four gins a night. He too fell into moods and flew into rages and punished her mother, mostly with verbal cruelty. She grew up in places I thought only I had been, and maybe that was part of the attraction.

The question cocks its head at every doorway, trying to see everything clearly, and remembering. In the field behind our small rented house in the Valley flatland when we came back from marrying, I am crouched under the fruit tree in the dark all a-tremble and I cannot hear her crying for my own. On the way home from a dinner party at the long straightaway by the East Stockton railroad crossing she turned to me at close range, driving because I could not, so deep behind my veil of drink and so certain of myself, hearing when I could no longer listen, and screamed from a face that was both desperate and pleading, "You are such a fucking asshole!"

I threw open the door then and threatened to jump onto the whizzing pavement until she stopped the car. The door slammed across the night and she went on alone, leaving me to my blind fury and the miles home, more than two hours of porch-lit Valley houses through the hard part of town, suicidal murderous intent let loose in me by what we barely restrained between us, hoping to pick a fight along the way. And at the end of the hall the memory turned back, its face a luminous dial in the darkness at the end, and it answered

   no

and this word rolling back past all those rooms into which I sent the messenger to ask, what was it, falling off the edge into lovemaking into a room of feeling so much larger than anything I had ever known, and that must be love, I thought then. But it was sex, too, and we were young and I thought it must be love that would last through anything, and later I wanted her to have a child while there was still time for her, I wanted the child too, our child, who came through the cut in her belly above legs deadened to all sensation and while she lay recovering I held the infant in my hands in the morning sunlight for her first tiny breaths.

   Emily

and can it ever recover, does it ever come back, come back from what it became to what it might have been?

   and the answer rolled back

   no.

You can't reheat a soufflé, my father said, with a shrug. He had an aphorism for just about everything.

Out here with Feo, lost in a fiction about anger and hope and betrayal, of people by people, and by circumstances and the unfolding of elements we never fully comprehend, I heard the answer and then heard myself cry out into the empty windless sails. I could not let my child slip away from me, despite pain of coming and going on weekends, constant reminders of the failure, whatever it was between her parents that they could not repair or did not choose to save, or perhaps never possessed to begin with, the courage or generosity or tolerance or capacity for forgiveness, all that must bind and hold people together over time.

If we lost our friendship in marriage we can reclaim it in divorce.

If we could not be happy together, at least we do not need to make each other unhappy apart.

Nothing dies between people that is not permitted to.

I had fallen asleep in the cockpit, trying to steer by intermittent shafts of moonlight striking down between clouds. The breeze came just before a red sunrise and by mid-morning was well up again.

Now perched on the forward hatch, my back to the mast, beer-froth foam breaking away from Feo's bow on both sides, I feel broken away. That voice that maligns me for not having written a novel as good as the one I have just finished, whose voice is that?

What does he want?

The voice that urges me on versus the voice that discourages, whose are those?

What would I find, if I went back through all my journals, back before I had Feo, and stopped to listen? Would I hear?

The ocean seems to rise vaguely to the north, a sloped plateau that cannot be.

The wind picked up to five on the Beaufort scale and the ocean came on in constant whitecaps atop overstuffed couches, marching en masse. The clouds bunched like bedclothes under the red sky at dawn, suggestion of stiffer breezes to come. We had made 66 miles overnight, and at 130 miles-a-day Feo was now within a week of Oahu.

I focused on nothing except shooting the sun and calculating our position. Hunched over the table with pencils and protractors and parallel rulers, I felt unfixed in this expanse of chart — unbalanced navigator with nerves on fire in a center of blankness, a stretch from continent to islands as long as my arm. I lost track of whether I had slept enough hours to think clearly, and only remembered to eat when I began to feel faint.

Just before midday I shot the sun 28 times in 37 minutes. It peaked at 83 degrees, 14.6 minutes above the horizon, local noon. It was 21 minutes and 24 seconds after the hour, corrected to Greenwich. An hour of computing produced a latitude and longitude that declared us to be 100 miles south of where I expected.

100 miles South?!

This position brought a wave of panic — 170 miles from yesterday's fix — impossible, given Feo's speed and direction through the night. The log recorded 138 miles.

Where were the other 32 miles? This fix declared us smack on the rhumb-line. The dots that had been marching predictably beneath the rhumb-line in the direction of Oahu had jumped way up above the line yesterday. Now they had come 100 miles down.

Impossible.

Obsessed with the mystery of it, I did not see the absurdity for some time. Halfway to Hawaii, I expected to know by now what I was doing. But obviously I did not. Being lost and confused now struck fear up into my arms, the feeling of suddenly hollowed bones.

The book said: if you get lost, just go south to the latitude you want; then go west.

Time and distance were on my side. There was nothing to run into *(what about a floating container?)*, just things to be run down by.

It only takes one.

The sun would keep going overhead every day.

If you can see it through the clouds.

I wrote a list of reasonable facts (I thought) to help lead me out of confusion.

If these two noon fixes were right, we had followed a compass course of 230 degrees for the last 24 hours.

The steering vane had held Feo in her grip throughout the night. The compass had been steady between 240 and 270 degrees. The wind had not shifted. We could not possibly have averaged 230 degrees.

Okay then, there must be something wrong with:

the sextant;

the compass;

the sights;

my calculations.

I stared. If each one were wrong then I was doomed. What was wrong with the noon shot? I reviewed all the numbers again and found no errors.

An idea seized me. The automatic course plotter! My father's beloved Director was a plastic navigational device that he had sent me for the trip, something he relied on in all his East Coast shoreline navigation. I had seen him use it time and again to bring us in fogbound weather to buoys invisible to the last. The Director promised to get dual monkeys off any navigator's back—variation and deviation.

The earth's shifting magnetic fields create a variation from geographic north, depending on your location. And the boat itself—particularly steel—can mislead the compass by small amounts, depending on your course. This is called deviation. My father first brought this phenomenon to my attention when I was 10 by surreptitiously placing his beer can beside the compass. In a few minutes it led me about 15 degrees off course.

"If you're going to drink, don't drive," he said with a laugh, a rule he frequently neglected to follow himself.

Every chart had a compass rose printed on it that showed True north and the degrees of magnetic variation at that location. (Moitessier's accounts of growing up in the South China Sea claimed that minute variations of magnetic pull could be felt by the Polynesians before they ever saw a compass or a British chart.) Here the chart showed a 14-degree variation to the east. Feo, heading southwest, produced 3 more degrees of easterly deviation: 17 degrees total.

So to follow the rhumb line of 240 degrees true to Oahu, I figured, we had to steer about 223 magnetic. I must have added variation to the compass course when I should have subtracted—an error worth 28 degrees!

But now I was not sure whether to subtract or add the variation to get the correct magnetic course.

The Director will lead me out of this.

Point the Director in the direction you want to go, it said on the box. Align the plotter arm with any vertical line on the chart.

Read the number in front of the little red arrow. That's your magnetic course.

The Director said I should be steering *Magnetic* 257 to be going a true 240. Not 223!

My body turned hot and cold. Something solid burned behind my eyes. I dug out Chapman's Piloting and reviewed the chapter on variation. Correcting from Magnetic to True, *add* easterly errors.

I have adjusted the stupid Director in reverse, but the stupidity is all mine.

Feo kept rocketing along, unmindful of the confusion in her belly. I went out into the cockpit and yelled into the rising wind:

"YEEEEAAAAAAAUUUUUNNNH!

The outburst released pressure under the edges of my skull. The ocean gave no sign of having heard.

I went below again and caught sight of the fix given by the Bohini. We were about 225 miles away from it, on a heading of about 240.

So, I thought, I have been right about the course.

I sensed there was something else amiss, but I hadn't the faintest idea what it was.

In the late afternoon I attempted another sun sight. But in the Almanac I selected a number from a column for Aries instead of the sun, then subtracted 141 from 187 and wrote down 146, an error that revealed itself because the tables couldn't respond to such absurd inputs.

"You fucking stupid idiot!" he yelled. I was alone in this cabin with someone who hurried and grew ever more anxious as he made these mistakes. He became his own worst problem.

I made tea and stared through the bubble at the oncoming white-topped waves. The sun had been starboard of the mast as I shot from the cockpit. We must be traveling south of west. The new line of position put us about 45 miles from the noon fix, twice as far as the log said we had traveled.

Blame the drift imposed by the wind and ocean currents, driving us at a southerly angle. It almost made sense, if I assumed the noon shot yesterday was nuts.

Don't lose faith in the compass, or the last noon sight, or the way you've figured the course all along.

Believe this noon fix.

Wait another day.

Don't worry.

T he seas charging from dead astern plunge Feo downhill into the trough ahead, then overtake and pass beneath her as she stalls on their departing backsides. The breeze seems to rise with the descent of evening and I am worried about an accidental jibe if a sea takes her stern suddenly across the wind. She must be making eight knots over the ground now, diving through her own thunderous bow wave. It is hard to judge on this downwind tack whether the mainsail needs a reef. A small shift in the vane turns Feo more across the wind to tip the gusts out of the sail as she rolls, and she settles into an easier gait.

Michel would let her fly with everything aloft, *Put them up and let God take them down.* I am not Michel, or anything like France's Eric Tabarly or Britain's Knox Johnson, but I know Feo has been here before, and then some. Through the portholes I watch the seas tower toward her before shouldering her out of the way. From time to time a wave erupts into a white heraldic pennant. It flutters with momentary pomp, then disappears into the distance.

What do you think all that upset is about? Brody asked.

I remember my mother leaving me in the hospital when they thought I had polio. I remember the hallway, the distance and the darkness as she went. Abandonment and terror. The fear of solitude is parallel. It has something to do with being away from her, losing that, or losing that forever.

What are you losing? What would you be losing of your mother?

A certain unqualified love. If I could actually wrench myself away, then maybe I could let myself be. Get away from this — this dependence, whatever.

You're dependent on her? Brody said.

Yes.

What do you think you might feel about her standing by when your father was beating you with that hose?

Brody sat up suddenly in his chair and grasped its arms with both hands.

She didn't intervene, did she? She didn't protect you. She was your mother. Was that unqualified love?

I've never really thought much about that, I said.

Maybe you should, he said.

The perfect silver coin of a moon disappears and reappears amid scudding purple clouds emblazoned gold at the edges. Phosphorescent sea creatures electrify the bow wave and illuminate Feo's path with pale green light, like a Palisades entryway into the night. The wind and seas are building as the moon climbs overhead to make this a wild, spot-lit ride through intermittent shafts of moonlight. Dark, cliff-like figures break alongside Feo to fill the cockpit air with spume. Her mast is pressed forward and tipped down, the bowsprit runs down to the far side of each rolling gully before turning up at the next crest like a maestro's giant baton keeping tempo. We are racing with the seas, backstays tight as piano wires, and I do not know what more to expect of this breeze. The clouds have an ominous winged look around the edges, speeding across the moon, sucked along and driven by some force whose excitement keeps rising. This ocean seethes, rushes onward, feeds on itself, spilling over into the dark ahead.

Phosphorescence flows helter-skelter across the deck until the lifelines drip a luminous green and Feo is driving across a field of pale campfires. She charges down one hill with a roar, pauses for a deep breath as the next sea rises beneath her stern, and collects herself for another swooping downward rush. I am braced in the cockpit, hand hooked under the hatch handle, charioteer to this thundering creature let loose by the wind and herded uproariously down these dark and fiery slopes.

I have lost track of time, of fear, and finally of myself.

Soon the wind has risen to a gale, hitting 40 knots in the gusts. Feo is moving at a breakneck pace with her rail rolled under time and again. Her plunging hull moves diagonally to these seas faster than I have ever sailed, mast cocked at 45 degrees to the water, the bow an upward-slicing knife into black space. She is spilling as much wind from the main as she can, I cannot stay awake much longer, staring to the horizon for freighters, fearing danger to the mast.

The cable cutters are ready in the port cockpit locker.

The seas loom above my head and several break onto the deck. I work my way forward in my harness to fight the main sail down past the sticking point. The boom thrashes. Feo pitches angrily, unwilling to reduce her sails, and her shrugging makes me feel ashamed.

We are down to mizzen and staysail. Feo's speed drops off, the seas swiftly overtake and outrun us. Water breaks along the gunwale and washes past the cabin and now I am too physically spent to go out onto the deck again. She descends into a vicious waddle and roll that will persist through the night. Muffled conversations arise from the bilge.

"*You!*" someone says.

"*What?*"

A loud thumping and stomping of feet. Voices echo in makeshift tunnels beneath me. The voices are drowned out by water thundering through huge pipes. Dishes clatter in the sink. Beneath me someone is banging his head against a water tank. Water is rushing all around. I wonder if I am beginning to show signs of fatigue.

You asked me what I thought when you said last time maybe you wanted to take a break from this, Brody said. I wondered what was going on with you.

I feel pretty good. I bought my own lap-top. I imagined I might become independent from the paper. I began to dream. What is the story in the notebooks I began to keep when I came aboard Feo? Where is the end? A friend called me to say she's going to sail to England this year. That inspired me to think more seriously about my own sailing and about her, or trying to live happily with a woman. My life's gone on and so has hers. Whatever was possible between us hit its limit. I have to decide — do I want it to happen? And if I do, how would that be?

You think it's that straightforward? Brody asked. You just decide?

Yeah, something like that.

Through the night of fitful bucketing I can hardly wait until dawn to get the mainsail back up again, double-reefed this time. The sky has collected into grey pillowcases on a distant clothesline and a looming, distended cloud releases a downpour amid violent gusts, but passes after a few minutes. I repair the cable between the wheel and the tiller and check the shrouds stem to stern. Record the overnight distance in the log. Inspect the bilge. I sit in a light rain with my back braced against the mizzen, palms warming around a cup of coffee, enveloped by occasional spray and the sound of waves rushing around the transom.

What was it one of the old hands said? Sailing alone in the ocean means days of anxiety interrupted by stretches of fear, punctuated by moments of sheer terror. The rest of the time you're just afraid.

I laughed aloud to remember it. Dealing with deep sentiments brings its own stretches of fear, like the elements. But the ineffable beauty of the sea is all around, all the time.

❀

I had begun to read *Habits of the Heart,* a book on individualism and commitment in American life sent along by my brother-in-law, a PhD in philosophy and part-time minister, as his way of communicating something he preferred not to say openly.

People who are too occupied by their own feelings are prone to such personal deviation and variation — to put it in compass terms — that they can never reach any intended destination. Perpetually en route, they never arrive. So they cannot be counted upon. Promises are not kept, contracts not honored. Marriages do not endure.

There is, the author was arguing, a lack of faith, no center. What does anyone believe anymore?

"How do I know there is a God?" My brother-in-law had queried his Maine congregation on a summer weekend when I went to visit in Hancock, a coastal town about an hour northeast of Cape Rosier.

"I lie down on the ground and look at a tree leaf," he said. "I find infinite complexity seeking order. In the process of evolution I see greater and greater complexity seeking more order, seeking greater complexity, and so on. I call that God."

"I hear a voice inside me all the time that knows me, that loves me, that cares about me, that wants the best for me. An honest voice that can't be deceived by me, that accompanies me, listens to me, is always there...and I call that God."

"I think I know that voice you were talking about," I said to him afterwards. "But what about that other voice, the one that says, I don't like you and don't trust you and I think you're an asshole? Is that the devil? If you were going to sermonize about that voice, what would you say?"

"That's a difficult question," he said. "I'll have to think about that."

Those negative voices were much more of a problem to me than that other voice. Whenever I could hear that first voice, I could respond to it.

A year or so later my brother-in-law still hadn't done the second sermon. He said he talked about it in a long letter to me, but somehow it got lost in the mail. He repeated again. It's a difficult question.

A small silver grey bird appeared, as round and plump and bright as an illuminated cloud. It flapped strenuously to stay aloft, with none of the powerful grace and calm of my earlier companion. With a desperate, inquisitive face it hurried on.

What am I doing out here? What am I up to, really?

I had gone back to see Joe Miller a second time to ask a few specific questions, trying to resolve confusion about a certain woman in my life. I said:

"If a man is looking for a perfect jewel and sees two that seem perfect but are very different, how does he decide which one is right for him?

"Neither one is right for him," said Joe. "The right one for him might contain elements of both."

"If he looks on a field of jewels and finds one that brings a great sense of calm, is that the right one?"

"That is the one that brings him a great sense of calm," said Joe.

At that moment the flock of birds that had been my feelings about my life and the people closest to me, uncertain about which way to go, suddenly collected en masse, and I felt them shift direction. Just the day before I had been talking to Brody about writing for myself again, and learning to forgive my father. Now I felt a moment of beginning arrive.

I passed through a membrane. It happened — clap! Just like that.

I took the taffrail log apart and oiled it and hung it back on the lifeline to keep recording our progress, turn by turn. I had now been alone for two weeks. I would not reach Hawaii before Emily was scheduled to fly back to the east coast with her mother. I would have to explain that sailors have destinations, not schedules. The trip to Hawaii I had promised her, to come meet me and Feo, would have to happen later, some other way. I hoped she would be able to understand.

A late afternoon shot gave me another line of position. The line from noon moved up 25 miles and the two lines intersected *exactly* where I thought I was. Exultant block capitals leaped into my journal:

"I KNOW WHERE I AM!"

I cooked a new ham and cheese casserole and cleaned the cabin. My handwriting and calculations were becoming neater and better organized every day. I put a reef in the mizzen and two in the main and checked all the lines for the night.

"*Don't worry*" said the Moon to the Stick Man with wild, curly-cue eyes, surrounded by charts and instruments.

"*Be Happy*" said the Sun. The Stick Man came out of his confusion into a day of blue waves and beautiful sailing. His small red craft edged into darkness toward a brilliant orange sphere that seemed to be smiling.

"Did I tell you I spoke
To the Man in the Moon?
His face came up like a shiny spoon
I said: "Gee, you look wonderful."
He said: "I always look this way in June."

The windlass sat silent and impenetrable in the foredeck. I stared at it and it stared back at me. The anchor swung gently in its chock over the bow and I examined the chain that ran aft from the anchor through the gears of the windlass and down into the chain-locker below deck. Feo kept forging south, clear about her own intention.

I stared out at the horizon and waited for some insight to dawn on me about how to release the windlass to drop the anchor. None came. In all my preparations it never occurred to me I would not know how to do this when the time came, and the time was coming. On a yellow legal pad, Angelica had scribbled the sort of explanation you might come up with in your second or third language.

"Anchor, safety pin, take little chain loose and pipe down to deck. Use pipe not hands. White paint mean chain almost over." The last three words were scratched out, followed by "red means-almost over."

"Block chain with sideways link. Tighten ... to raise: pipe in white tube @ rear > pump."

I reread her words again and again. Something in the windlass gears had to be released for the chain to run, but what? I pushed and prodded every part, stuck the pipe into any hole it would fit in, and heaved this way and that. Nothing.

I could tighten the chain up but there seemed to be no way to let it down. So 150 feet of it — hundreds of rusty pounds coiled below decks — would have to be released somehow by hand at the moment of anchoring — a potentially dangerous prospect, going into a strange harbor alone.

What are you thinking? Brody asked.

Ah, about pain. Background noise, like headaches. When you feel one, you can't imagine not feeling one. That's the nature of some experiences. I will find a way to work things out.

Is the need to get this these things resolved connected to the need to prove yourself, do you think? Brody asked. Whether you accept it or not, your family still carries that gene of, "things need to be perfect."

Yes, I suppose so.

When you were growing up as the youngest of three, were you trying to impress them? And also trying to decide: is this who I am, or is that who I am?

The windlass was not about to divulge its secret. I sat in the bowsprit with my journal and made the only entry I would ever make at 29 degrees North, 144 West, above 14,000 feet of water. The ocean now seemed to tip southwest into the afternoon sun, making things easier. Feo was washing along at six knots, the Pacific endless and spotless all around, with a sky to match.

I t is theoretically possible from the deck of a sailboat to spot Mauna Kea and Mauna Loa, rising above 13,000 feet like misshapen pyramids, at a distance of about 125 miles. The pair would rank as the largest mountains on earth if measured from the ocean floor — a lesser-known fact about the "Big Island" of Hawaii. The volcanic archipelago extends 1,400 miles in a narrowing band of 130 islands to the northwest, but nearly the entire landmass, a Polynesian kingdom until 1893, is found among the first eight. Less than 700,000 years old, these are the earth's youngest offspring.

The Big Island anchors the entire chain, with Maui, Kahoolawe, Lanai and Molokai extending from it in a tight elliptical array. Then come Oahu, Kauai, and the little satellite Nihau that is out-of-bounds for non-Hawaiians. These seven lesser islands appear on the map as an odd jigsaw puzzle, which if pieced together would comprise a facsimile of the Big Island.

Because I had planned to motor up Honolulu's narrow, reef-lined channel into Oahu, I had one chart for all eight islands, but detailed charts only for Oahu and Kauai, where I expected to go to prepare for the return trip. Now, with no engine or running lights, I could not get into Oahu safely.

The trade winds that prevail from the east and northeast through most of July strike Mona Loa first, throwing up a camouflage of cloud and haze along the horizon and often rendering the land invisible to the very last. Crossing the islands the winds sweep off the headlands to gust fiercely just offshore, like williwaws known to hit with deadly force off the promontories in Australia.

Hilo, the second largest and best protected port in the chain, lies roughly in the middle of the Big Island, and offers the most convenient target for any sailboat without power. Heavy rain was common — 130 inches a year — but violent storms were rare. Only eight thunderstorms had hit the year before, and it was considered unlikely that any typhoon would reach the islands from the western Pacific. But the Pilot said to watch out for the *Mumuku*, powerful offshore winds crossing the southwestern coast between Keahole and Upolu Points. I did not expect to pass that way.

Charley's Charts of Hawaii, a cruising pamphlet that outlines Hawaii's limited natural harbors, warns against using its renderings for navigation or to approach the shore.

"Mistakes are most easily made when fatigue and excitement build after many days at sea," said Charley. Ignorance was normally at fault when sailors ran aground in this warm water. The corals that spread out in reefs from shore would outdate any chart over time.

Tropical reefs have a life of their own. Vessel traffic is heavy, scan every 15 minutes.

If only I had more charts. But who ever prepares for the truly unexpected?

Michel's charts were stored beneath the port berth in the aft cabin, untouched for months. I wrestled them out, about 50 pounds worth of French and British admiralty renderings, some dating back to the last century. (How much *does* coral grow in 100 years?) The dank smell of old paper filled the humid cabin. Endless islands and coastlines unfolded beneath my hands, shadows of underwater mountain ranges as mysterious as they were wide and deep. Mexico and Central America went back into storage, but others drew me into their folds. Michel's years with Feo emerged in bits and pieces, in no particular order.

He left Tuamotu heading south to the Society Islands, Tahiti, Moorea, Raiatea, Tahaa, and then went west to Bora Bora.

Upolu, Western Samoa, Viti Levu in Fiji, on to New Caledonia in the New Hebrides.

Occasional tissue tracings of inshore passages, where he might have copied another navigator's directions, fell out of larger charts. Feo's sounds of motion stirred the rudder-post beneath me, a deep clanking sound. She had steered him to all these places, or he had steered her.

Some were clean and unmarked, others catalogued his noon sights and star shots. Here, his irregular path across the remote barrier islands above the Tropic of Capricorn in 1984. Here, a detail of Espiritu Santo Island in the New Hebrides, from a French survey conducted in 1892, a line showing his entrance into tiny Hog Harbor on the eastern shoulder. How did that coastline finally appear as he approached, this ancient drawing his only image of what waited for him?

I was trying to find a bus to the end of Market Street and the outer Mission District. The first driver sent me to the next stop and a cluster of people took the stairs of a pedestrian overpass to cross the street. I followed them to a tunnel leading out onto a distant field. Ambiguous signs and flashing lights seem to encourage but also prohibit my entrance. Small obstacles along the way, like a version of pedestrian speed bumps, seem to carry live electricity. I followed the path to find myself alone in a large open field, isolated from the urban activity. The field had been made over with some kind of sensing devices.

A phone rang from the surface of the ground nearby. I sat and watched the golden space, like a wheat plain in the embrace of mountains. Solitude here was perfect but suffused with a much larger presence, oddly mechanical and technical. It anticipated me but it seemed utterly indifferent. I know I must return to the passageway by whatever route I can find. I observe myself walking among land mines.

I did not arrive back at the beginning place, but awoke with a sense that crucial elements in my life were converging in ways yet to be understood.

Daring and endurance stretched across these pages as Michel went deeper into remote regions. The charts seemed to emit his courage as they catalogued Feo's experience with him. The Maldives, Madagascar, Cape Town, anchorages in the Cook Islands, grey etchings with French headings, crude drawings that recorded good holding ground.

Isla Cla—ion. Water stains obscured several letters. This was the passage, but which was the island?

Here across the tiny islands of Tuamotu, the northwest passage toward Motu Tuga, the Passe Tapuhiria between Patagahiti and Turuki, tiny white spaces in the coral noting "boat passage..." Here was the angular Suwarrow Island. A photocopy of the Canton Islands. Now Palmyra, Christmas, the Wallis Islands.

His chart markings grew more and more familiar. He always etched his noon fix with the same deft cross, slightly askew. One after another, nothing to do with Hawaii, they drew me along, aroused the reporter who had never left the comfort of his own culture long enough to lose himself in the wilds.

The rented motorcycle had brought me from the beach in Phuket along the coastal gravel road where it turned up into the Thai jungle. I began imagining local tigers and the twisted road. How far was I now from anyone and anything, how unknown would this side trip be to anyone who might ever come looking for me? No one would ever find my body on this high gravel path, gutted by early monsoon. I turned back then toward the small,

thatched, beachfront town and returned the motorcycle, just an-
other journalist on vacation in Thailand, hurrying to meet a for-
mer university colleague for dinner at the hotel.

Here the chart declared patches of "dangerous ground,"
incompletely surveyed areas of the South China Sea, spots of
"discolored water," magnetic anomalies that could not be explained. An island relocated by as much as five miles in 1971,
correction from an 1892 survey.

The Gulf of Siam, Marine Hydrographic Service of Paris,
1866; Mekong Delta, 1925, warning of pirates between Phu-
Quoc and the Balua Islands. Did he expect to enter here? Had
he come this far? What did he think he would find?

Bangkok Harbor, 1931. Etchings of island passages in Fiji,
where it was difficult to distinguish between the end of the
water and the onset of land, or between passable depths and
dangerous reefs. Navigators note: positions could not be trans-
ferred between charts because of inconsistent latitude and longitude markings.

The navigator is advised to locate himself by sighting objects
on land.

He closed in on Urukthapel Island from the east, in the
early morning hours. Here were star shots of Vega and Pisces
near Rarotonga, as he sailed across French Polynesia in 1981.
Dutch surveys of the Molucca Sea, 1931, south of Celebes; the
Nicobar Islands in the Bay of Bengal; D'Entrecasteaux Islands
east of Papua New Guinea; the Sulu archipelago off Borneo.

If he had traveled them all, he had not marked them all.
Certainly he could not have traveled them all.

"L'enfant perdu," a sudden sharp rock off the entrance to Cayenne on the east coast of French Guyana, 1867 rendering. The lost child.

The French in translation jumped out at me in the voice of my Godmother, Aunt Mary. She had been my mother's closest friend since before I was born, and never missed my birthday or failed to acknowledge Christmas where I was concerned. She had sprinkled notes of encouragement or advice throughout my life whenever she thought I needed it.

"Don't sail away from your little girl, she needs her Dad. Find yourself a good dame and settle down," Mary had written, in mild protest to the news that I was planning to sail to Hawaii on my own. Bundled in sweat clothes aboard Feo as I recuperated from pneumonia, I was typing a reply to her on Michel's old manual machine, surrounded by radio jazz and the litter of recent correspondence and several unfinished short stories as winter rain pelted the hatches.

Among the conflicted voices saying, "Do this!" "No, what about this?" one voice had tried to confront the unhappy marriage but could not make itself heard in the din. Maybe sailing to Hawaii would be sailing away from everything, and not towards anything. But some desires that well up from the deep might emanate from your true spirit, composed of fragments, trying to realize itself.

"No, Aunt Mary, I am trying to get back to the thing that brought me to newspaper writing in the first place. I will not desert my child."

Michel had anchored in Resolution Bay on Saint Christina Island. In Tuamotu he had used star shots to close in on the islands, and his lines advanced toward the small up-croppings in parallel. In Nukuhiva, in Marchand Island in the Marquesas, I could see from a small penciled cross that he had anchored where a trio of valleys — Oata, Havao and Pakiu — converged into a horse-shoe cove called Taiohae.

Successive anchorages were marked along the southern edge of southeastern Tahiti, a tomato-shaped aneurysm off its lower right corner. Here the Timor, Arafura, Sawoe and Banda seas, north of Australia. In Western Australia, the transcontinental railroad crossed the high desert Plain of Nullarbor, through Kalgoorlie and on to Toodyay.

The Hearst newspaper empire was declining under the weight of family conflicts, a vast inheritance becoming just another American corporation of the '80s, a machine with a weakened heart and soul increasingly difficult to identify. Old man Hearst's political obsession had lost its fire. Jack London's hometown newspaper, once synonymous with adventure itself, was now constrained within limited newswires and the imperatives of corporate advertising. Few fresh voices came in or managed to emanate forth. What was the Big Idea? The implicit contract was: work within these corporate confines and be unsatisfied.

Or withdraw in search of your own joy.

The Gilbert Islands from an American survey in 1841 and a German survey in 1875. How much coral might have grown since *then*?

Coast of Spain, Cadiz, Barcelona. The Mediterranean across southern France, past Marseille. I traced tiny coastline details, difficult to follow now in Feo's motion as seas began to build from the northeast. My eyes went in search of Villefranche, amid print almost too tiny to read, where I turned 21 on a beach with a local girl who left behind only a book of matches and a memorable indentation in the sand.

Michel had drawn his own compass rose in the middle of the Mediterranean, red and green colored pencil marks alternating every five degrees. He crossed from Gibraltar through the Canaries in 1973, 30 days across the Atlantic to Barbados, the point to which he would return in 1976, having rounded the Horn alone. That's where he rolled over with Feo, standing on her cabin ceiling in the dark until she rolled back, and then sailed up the other side of the continent.

"What is most scary is hearing the surf along the coral beaches at night when you are not able to go in, not able to leave or turn back because there are reefs all around. You sail up and down along the white line in the dark and listen to the surf and you wait for morning. This is the scariest place," he said.

The skin on Angelica's face drew back as he spoke of this during the one dinner we had together on Feo, where the smell of roast lamb and his stories and Angelica sitting close by were enough to convince me of just about anything.

Here were anchorages in western Nicaragua, El Salvador, and another Farallon Island off Ilse Orchilla, north of Caracas. He tacked at night off the north coast of Panama.

A meandering path through the Grenadines, Union Island, Tobago Cays, Cannouan in October of 1974, tiny Pigeon Island to the north. Here was Antigua as surveyed by a Captain E. Barnett in 1848, exactly a century before my birth.

In falling ill, what is it that you are really sick of? Brody asked. And how do you intend to heal?

Hoping to get away on the boat, be truly alone. Face the elements, discover whether I can endure. All of these things are converging — the conversations with Joe, you, the turmoil, everything. I don't know where it all comes out. I have only just started to listen to my heart and challenge the things that scare me. I'm frightened to think any one woman might be the right woman for me. I'm afraid of repeating past mistakes or believing something is true when it isn't or discovering that she will betray me.

If I step out into my own true desire — it's such a long way to fall. I've got so many chips on the table now. It's scary to make the bet. Still I say, okay, roll the card over. I want to see it.

Canal of Birds, Nonesuch Bay.

These charts came out in no particular order, Italy, San Remo to Vada, the Canal de Piombino. Black and grey etching took on the shape of a giant insect, head poised over something edible, another island beneath the peninsula that was the insect's body.

The Straits of Magellan penetrated a stretch of dazzlingly complex islands, interwoven feathers under a giant wing of land, interstices clustered around that disintegrated base of South America, from Patagonia to Tierra del Fuego. The famous inland passage followed one reach after another — Sea, Long, Crooked, English, Froward, rounding Mt. Victoria at 53/54 South latitude, 71 degrees west Longitude, then turning through Famine and Broach reaches, up to Dungeness, on the eastern corner. Michel had chosen the long way around, over the Everest of oceans.

In the beginning of his 14 years at sea, from Portsmouth to the Canary Islands and the Azores, he marked the compass rose coming out of the Mediterranean into the Atlantic, showing the course from Gibraltar through the Canary Islands. So, setting out into our first ocean, our courses had been the same, 240 degrees.

One sight reduction after another riddled his passage through the Canaries, faint marks suggesting that his, too, were repeated over and over, then erased.

At the end of searching for any chart that might help me now, I found only the west coast of Hawaii, from Cook Point to Upolu on the west and another pair showing the western halves of Molokai and Lanai. Kealakekua Bay, Captain Cook's original anchorage and eventual burial place, was one option on the far side of Hawaii but it made no sense to sail all that way around.

Lanai, fully owned by Castle and Cook for Dole Pineapple production, last vestiges of the plantation economy, was only fifteen miles long and 10 miles wide. It had nothing to show but a tiny harbor called Kaumaulapau. The detailed inset described a few moorings and well protected holding ground of six fathoms in an area about the size of a football field.

Hilo would be a sure source of engine repair, well marked by Peepeekio Point lighthouse eight miles to the north. Clear sailing downwind to the head of the Bay and the harbor. Swells would break on the outer reef during heavy trade winds. The Coastal Pilot warned of powerful currents and devious chop where the trade winds struck the black lava cones at Kumukahi to the east and divided along the island shores.

Beware of night entry, better to stand off 'til dawn.

I followed the tracks of summer hurricanes that had struck out from Mexico in recent years. Only four storms since 1950 had retained their power all the way through the islands. In 1982, the last bad year, Hurricane Iwa came up out of the south and crossed Kauai on the way northeast. In July, Gilma diminished to a tropical storm as she came west at 145 west longitude, and petered out well south of Hawaii. Daniel faked south and then hooked north between Hawaii and Maui. In August, Kristy and John remained hurricanes all the way to 150 West Longitude before they faded away. Even if it only got close, a hurricane of moderate force could drive dangerous wind and waves through the island channels.

"What about rogue waves?"

My father, a lifelong student of arcane dangers, from killer bees to meteor showers, had read of waves six stories high that swept an ocean freighter's decks clean — cargo containers and superstructure — everything stripped bare. In fact, a Japanese sailor from Tokyo had come single-handed into San Francisco a few months before I left with a tale of leaping up his mast in mid-ocean as a three-story wave advanced on him and broke over the deck as he clung to the lower spreader. The most recent tsunami to strike Hawaii had been 1960, when 61 people died in Hilo Bay.

You can't worry about rogue waves.

Charley's guide included a polished photo of placid water in Hilo's Radio Bay with a yacht standing still at anchor. I was looking forward to the Suisan Fish auction, where the guidebook said giant tuna are carved like sides of beef, and the Liliuokalani Gardens, Japanese style.

Go slowly into unfamiliar waters.

T he morning sun worked its way up a sky of exploded mountains while the seas advanced like blue-grey bison thundering across woven slopes of plain. They rose and declined on larger undulations of the deep, herds of dark heads and white horns tossed upwards at the moment their animal shapes could be seen at close range. Then they were off with the swift unfold of wind that had driven them so forcefully to this place.

I had wakened several times after midnight and gone on deck to feel the rollers building, thankful now to have taken in the staysail and reefed the mizzen before dark. Feo might not be making all the speed she could but I was sleeping easier during the night.

Even with shortened sail we covered 140 miles over 20 hours, the fastest sustained pace to this point. The white foam thundered wide from Feo's bow and her hull shuddered with thick and staccato sounds. I felt so tuned to her I no longer distinguished her sensations from my own.

Sun-sights promised to grow more difficult.

Feo is high and low and twisting on the gleaming backs of these bison, the horizon escapes in the wink of an eye. I am not sure if what I see through the tiny mirror is horizon or bison shoulder.

I have almost screwed the glittering disk to the horizon when another bison looms, or Feo swings across a steep wave, and the vane hauls her back. She has put the mizzen into my view at the wrong instant. I am too early or too late.

I am braced at the top of the companionway, notebook tucked behind the hatch cover, pencil in my teeth, eyes in deep ache from squinting into the glare. The sun is a diving grouse in the woods of Ganges, I see my father raise his shotgun with a grace that conceals its speed. The barrel rises and barks and the winged brown ellipse falls in a puff toward the running retriever's open mouth. I am hunting another celestial bird that does not swoop and dive, it is Feo plunging along in a seething hiss of abandon. The galvanized orb through the filtered lens will not touch, refuses to touch, swings too deep below a line that was not horizon after all.

No, not there, not yet, there, that was almost it, yes that was it, just then.

Time!

My digital watch stares back with its square limpid eye.

If I am wrong, when will I know? I need to know now more than ever.

The first morning shot and reduction and plotting had been riddled with errors. I had added a degree of latitude and thrown the computation into nonsense. The sextant had developed an error, a sign of wear easily corrected, but I kept forgetting to include it in the calculation. The day before I had taken three shots three minutes apart and did not understand why the lines of position should be parallel, and all so close together. Much later I would see this confusion as evidence I was not yet qualified to be navigating alone at sea.

Snorting, shaking, jostling, they shoulder their way in long lines, horns askew, eyes ablaze, great rumps catching sun sheen on their backs. The horizon to the northeast spews them forth continuously, fugitives from the sun teeming southwest to the far edge of ocean.

To reduce the chance of missing the islands altogether, I had been shooting for the middle of the chain that stretched in a band 300 miles across my path. Turning towards Hilo meant I had to change course by 20 degrees further south and aim for the Big Island. Still making errors of 30 or 40 miles at a time — one line of position had me 64 miles from my presumed location — I was aware that I might miss my target. A single-hander from Oregon the previous summer had missed the islands in just this way and put himself into the deep ocean. After 70 days and three weeks without solid food he surfaced at a distant atoll as a surprise to his wife, who had given him up for lost.

I am not sure how to manage the fear of my own uncertainty.

They rear up on arrival, startled by the sight of this red and white angular creature not themselves. Some dart to one side, others roll underneath. The most powerful bucks in full rut rise to their full height and rage in speckled froth, rearing up to strike with seething white conical heads, wild unicorns with swollen horns of emerald ink. In a rising flood the leader explodes and falls back into the herd, jostling to get by. Froth descends into a trembling gorge, swept on as swiftly as it arrives.

*H*ow was it, not coming for a few weeks? Brody asked.

The currents and crosscurrents are pretty intense. I'm not sure I want to be completely alone with them. I have to work it out myself. I haven't gotten to the end.

So doing it on your own is moving away from me, from someone who helps you look at this?

I want to feel I'm getting there myself. I know I'm getting there alone, even if you help me.

It also has to do with intimacy, too.

(Auto horns in the distance).

Do you perceive me as an angry person who is afraid of intimacy and is on a doomed course?

I wouldn't say doomed. A course you wouldn't want to be on.

I feel I've got to stop and think: do I dislike women?

I don't think we said dislike, we said angry. That also gets into dependence, independence, anger. Maybe you have to feel your way more.

A couple of fast connections go off when you say that: feelings about my mother, that I don't want to be in her web. What is the web? I am subject to a deal: that I will love you but you can never leave me. It feels like a trap or subjugation. I am being owned. That's the fear of intimacy. I don't want to feel hemmed in and controlled or contained and possessed.

Is she like that, your mother?

I don't think she would say that.

What would she say?

She'd say, I don't know what you're talking about.

What about from your perception?

I see myself saying to her: 'I can't be what you want me to be for you.'

(Long pause.)

A recent magazine article described research into a pattern that was fairly common in the 1950's. Some women used a son to provide what they weren't getting from their husbands and marriages — companionship, emotional intimacy, whatever. It made me think back to my early teens, and before that, when my

---

mother and father were fighting. These fights would start out of nowhere and get vicious, usually after he was into the evening drinking. An eruption over nothing. The scenes would repeat over and over. He would accuse, she would deny, he would insult or browbeat her until she cried, threaten to kill himself, storm off. I don't think he ever hit her that I know of. He taught us that you never ever hit a woman. I was the last child, my brother and sister had gotten out. I was just trying to keep her happy and maintain her spirits. Looking back on it I guess she was using me to replace what wasn't there for her. Of course he hated that. That was the way it really was, but I had never thought of it that way. I had no idea what was really going on, really.

My plotting sheets were no longer marred by erasures and points nearly falling off the edge of the page, or one line failing to intersect the only other one that could make sense of our position. I had begun to catch my own errors as I made them. A sun shot from an hour before noon, advanced six miles to the noon position, made a fix exactly where I expected to be, near the center of the bull's-eye.

Have faith you can work your way to the answer.

Practice, Persistence, Patience, Perseverance.

These four P's lined up in the log, joined a moment later by a fifth. I forgot to adjust for a five-second watch error, gained on Greenwich Mean Time, and worth 20 miles or so.

Pride goeth before a fall, my mother liked to say.

Three noon fixes in a row now pointed a straight arrow at Hilo, on a course of 225 degrees True. The most recent put Feo 360 miles away, west of the Gulf of Alaska, about even with the midlands of Mexico. From the straight line trend I grow calmer. I am going to believe my noon shots.

Flying fish burst from the wave-tops like hordes of small helicopters with rotors on both sides. I adjusted the wind-vane for a course on the Maui side of Hilo. If I missed the Big Island, I wanted to hit some island, any island.

P resent No. 3 from my sister was a tape cassette, out of which her teenage daughter's mid-western twang reverberated humorously into the other music of cabin sounds: wire mesh vegetable holder banging against the cabin wall, stove clanking in gimbals, thunderous water tank collisions down below, gallons ricocheting in Feo's hold.

"I remember you singing *My Country Tis of Thee* at the top of your lungs in Maine," she said, "so here goes." From her tremulous alto sax came the slightly labored melody, halting and saddened, full of breath and effort.

She followed with *Amazing Grace*, her mother's favorite.

"It's hotter than the hinges of hell out here in Chicago, about 95 degrees," she said. "Have a good time on your cruise, expedition, voyage, whatever you call it. I hope you have a better sense of direction than my father. P.S. Here's a song he said you like."

The voice of Aretha Franklin burst into the cabin and brought the late '60s along with her in a rush

"Think! Think, think, think about what you're trying to do to me, oh think, think, think... oh let yourself be free..."

I was suddenly up and dancing on Feo's narrow floor-boards, which were cresting, tilting, rising, rocking back and forth like a giant surfboard

"Oh, Freedom..."

and the movement of the floor became the movement of my feet, on a boat you climb a rising floor but try not to descend, making gravity your ally

"Freedom..."

because you are more stable going uphill than down, when it changes direction you stop — until it sets itself in motion again — and then you move to it

"Freedom..."

and Feo was dancing with me, she was the cabin and I was in her and

"Freedom!"

I could see myself in the small mirror between the port-holes, my arms and legs more tanned and muscled than I remembered, grinning, Brazilian fist and amber bead against my chest on the yellow twine, clicking to the music, beard coming on darkly and the ocean came and went around us to Aretha and the squeak of wet sneakers on the cabin floor and we danced until I was drenched

"Freedom!"

And a voice announced, "This Is WJMK the voice of Chicago's golden-oldie station, Happy Birthday Sweet 16!"

I sat staring at the windlass again, waiting for it to give me some hint of its inner workings. And then my sister said, in the voice that had always been ready to talk or listen,

"I hope whatever problems have come along have been easily solved, after the initial terror. We'll be overjoyed to hear from you. Give a holler out in the middle of the ocean. Maybe it will float all the way back to Chicago."

Childhood confidante, no one knew more family secrets than she did, and I knew some of hers. Whenever they fought, she hid upstairs in her room, a pillow held tight over her head as she crouched under the covers.

"You couldn't give less of a bloody damn about me." His voice is seething with rage and hatred. "Not a bloody damn."

"Vincent, don't be ridiculous." She is trying to sound reasonable but the tremble is in her voice and we can only imagine exactly where they are in the house, driven from room to room by the flow of his anger. A door slams like a gunshot to leave the voices half-muted and muddled.

"Not ridiculous! Damn well a fact, and you know it."

"Not! I most certainly do not!!"

Her voice cracks and we can both picture the stricken look around her mouth, her eyes shocked and tearful. He already has three stiff bourbon old-fashioneds in him, or maybe more depending on how long ago he started, but she is not far behind, because whatever he makes for himself he almost always makes one for her too. His fists are clenched like his jaw muscle, which puts a grim edge of brutality on his face. Maybe he has already jerked his overcoat out of the kitchen coat closet and gotten out his keys, ready to make for the door. If the sounds of him storming out — the back door by the shed and the front door under the stairs have two completely different sounds, it depends on where he left his car in the driveway — do not include one of those doors slamming, with the sound of the Buick soon to follow, we will not move from where we are.

I never thought my sister really knew what to make of the abusive sounds down below in that old house, even as she got older. They left her to cry alone in her room. Nothing would ever be said about whatever had happened downstairs, which could turn the house into an atmosphere of silent recrimination and dread for days at a time. Once my brother had gone off to boarding school he was out of it. She soon followed and then I was left alone with them for several years before I started to find my own way out.

I held the microphone close to prevent the wind from drowning me out.

"Besides getting the rigging snarled and losing the engine and lights and Loran, I'm trying to figure out the mechanism to release the anchor chain, so I don't have to sail in with 150-feet coiled on deck and throw it overboard at the last minute. I'll probably end up like Gregory Peck's Ahab in the death scene, dragged down by one bad error.

"But listen..."

I held the microphone over the edge of the bow.

"Listen to the sound of the bow wave. It's late afternoon. The sea is the color of new lead and you can see in the clouds whatever you like — knotted ropes, moss hanging on a stone face, butterflies, apparitions set free at last... Listen to the long and short torn cadence of the bow wave, snorting, tearing, widening, falling... The sprawl of the sky is like the spread of the sound, the texture of the cloud is like the foam beneath."

The thought of her now filled me up and I said to end the tape:

"You are one in a million and the world is lucky to have you in it. The ocean is so beautiful in her many faces and I am blessed to be here. If I have one idea to pass along, it would be this: Dream your dream, and go do it."

It was overcast when I turned in. The Stick Man sent messages on the wind, fiercely blown by a frowning cloud. "I Love You Emily!" he cried. "Can you hear me?" Feo sailed on with the Stick Man lying happily on the deck, his legs crossed, and the bubble above his head proclaimed: "Just Thinking."

There could be no more sublime place to be than among these ocean currents, magnetic fields shifting mile on mile between the earth's poles. Feo's hull would be realigned to her original magnetic identity by the time we returned.

It occurred to me then for the first time: Coming out to get free and clear, I might come back free. Maybe even clear.

I woke to an eerie shrillness to see distended clouds chasing Feo down explosive seas, the platinum moon in pursuit across a darkly shattered windshield sky. The night had a slight edge. I went back below to make coffee and put sweat clothes on under my foul weather gear.

The clouds rose above us like shutters on a high wall, closing against an infinite window of stars. The moon illuminated distant wave tops and then disappeared and we went on with darkness above and tiny star twinkles along the horizon. The bright night sky vanished under a cone of black, with nothing left but the shrillness growing thinner.

I crawled forward to take the jib down and instantly the wind fell. Feo lost speed and I hoisted the jib back up. The wind came right back up and sudden raindrops thrummed on the cabin tops to fill the air with mist. Then it stopped. A faint darkening of the water that was rain ran off into utter blackness. The wind came audibly into the silence that had been there moments before. The heavens split down the middle, rain to the west and moonlight to the east, and Feo tracked straight down the spine of a divided night sky.

The vane danced and kept Feo happily on her downwind course and I scanned the horizon. They would be coming from the port side out of Mexico, and dead aft from San Francisco down their rhumb-line to Hilo. Surely they must come down from Vancouver as well. In the rain I would not see their lights or hear them coming.

There, a flare at the horizon!

No, it is only a shooting star. I would be pursued like this for several more nights. I should keep watch but I could not keep constant watch. I would have to do the best I could and then give myself up to fate. If chance was going to claim me under a freighter's bow, so be it.

You do not stay healthy by worrying about cancer.

My head began drooping after midnight as Feo heaved up and down with the slow rhythm of my breathing. I went below to sleep, only to be rolled up against the cabin wall by sudden gusts. In one instant I jumped awake to see giant spotlights sweeping through the portholes, great scythes of light cutting back and forth through the cabin,

My God a freighter is on me!

and I jumped out of the berth, caught the galley pole with one hand against a downward roll and hoisted myself up the steep cabin floor to look out through one porthole to see no freighter but a black night sky and ragged silvery cloud pulled back as the moon drenched this patch ocean with bright steel. Its light slashed the cabin like a polished cutlass.

"You're out of your mind," my father said. I pictured him sitting in the wrinkled gray pajamas that matched the pale white of his hair, the fourth day in the St. John's hospital after they tried to stabilize his heart the first time.

"I'm going to come out of this," he said. He used that quiet tone that could make you believe whatever he said, and I believed him. And he was right, against all their odds and predictions. He quit drinking because the doctor said he must, and he made it look as straightforward as throwing a light switch, the only example I had ever seen that made me think I could do the same.

"It's simple," he said. "It's a matter of deciding."

If he died while I was out here, would I feel a signal? The sea has only her wind and waves and perfect indifference. Whatever path you choose will lead to a different place from the one you imagined. That is the nature and the power of letting go.

Experience is the best teacher, he always said — that, and trying to teach something to others that you want to know more about. Sometimes you will find the most important thing is what you didn't know you didn't know.

*G*o see Hoosiers, *I said to Brody. The father is a drunk and his son is the town high school basketball star. The father loves basketball and loves the son. But he can't escape the booze or the hold it has on him. He stumbles out into the basketball* court in the middle of the game and yells at the referee, and then is escorted off the floor, humiliating his son on the most public ground. Later, the boy visits the father in the sanatorium and stares at him for a long time. Finally, with a hint of sympathy and resignation, he says:

"I love you, Dad."

What I have tried to describe to you before — that overpowering feeling, something physically larger than I am trying to get out of my body, came up now, as much solid as liquid, trying to break out of me. I thought I might throw up or crack open right there in the theater, it was a struggle to keep silent and not fall out of my seat.

What do you think that is? Brody said.

It must have come from all the times I faced him when he was beside himself, all his fury focused on me. My mother was in another room crying, or withdrawn, capitulated. He seemed so full of hatred and cruelty and meanness. I didn't really know what it was about. But I must have felt that I was defective, or that I must have done something terribly wrong to deserve this from my father. How could he be wrong? I must be wrong. Now watching the boy in Hoosiers come before his father and stand there and forgive him — I guess I felt all those things at once, anger...

Anger and...? Brody repeated.

Anger and frustration and rage and humiliation and love and — and forgiveness, trying to realize itself.

I'm not sure that you're ready to forgive him, Brody said.

That's why I said what I said, forgiveness trying to become itself. I think maybe — a girlfriend asked me recently, what do I really want to do with my life, and the answer was I want to write. Yet something has always stood in the way. Because of what I have felt I couldn't say...

(Sound of sobs)

...while he was alive.

Why?

(Long silence.) It's too painful, too irretrievable. In his waning years he doesn't need to know. He wouldn't know what to do with it. He couldn't.

The day's tape ended there. I remember I was trembling, with tears streaming down my face. I was aware of Brody witnessing something that had never emerged before, not even to me — beginning to give in to those feelings, hoping to release them all, once and for all.

My father had never escaped that pale green office cubicle at the Lowell Gas Company on East Merrimack Street, half paneling and half glass, that he occupied for nearly 30 years. He occasionally took me there on Saturday mornings because he had work left to do, he said, and as far as I could tell, he was the only one there who regularly came in on that extra morning. He never made good on a single furious threat — that he would quit the little utility company that never promoted him, or that he would take his own life with the .22, or "just bloody disappear." No, in the end he stayed in the job and his marriage and made sure the three of us got the college education he never had, and taught us more than we knew. Maybe by venting his rage on us he could live with the demons that drove him to it, or at least hold them at bay. And there had to be a price.

By dawn the seas had built to three times Feo's height, running an equal distance apart, peak to peak. They exhorted her down their steep faces, pale blue sky and pearl white clouds rolling southwest over our course. A flat swirl beside us would rise like an oil tank without cylindrical restraints, confused

---

about whether it was solid or liquid. The tank would appear and dissolve in an in-taken breath, an apparition that quickly disappeared downhill in the confusion of those seas. Gusts marked the ocean surface with a wrinkled sense of fleeting time and impatient clouds came over in droves, clumps of un-raked leaves or sun-bleached cattle skulls in the desert.

The wind rose above 30 knots through the afternoon, a whistling gale. The seas grew to about 15 feet high, not sharp and abrupt but rounded conical intruders from a new and different ocean. I did not fear waves now as much as see something to read in them. But I had never seen waves like this and did not know what to make of them.

Giant potato heads. Feo lunged around a face below a nose and through a neck along the shoulder before another rose up behind. The shoulder she rides above becomes another faceless head beside her. She is wallowing among a few clustered figures before pushing herself out into a clearing. We are jostled along by a restless crowd, urging itself downhill.

The bottom edge of the jib cuts a triangle above the horizon, the mainsail taut along the mast. I sit at the foot of the mast and watch the masthead tipping forward as the boom touches the water to leeward on every deep roll. Someone in the boatyard warned that I would be able to see the upper part of the mast bend just before it exploded.

I see it now!

No, the bend is not there. This mast is too big to break. I saw it naked before I refinished it, and it has no weak points. I tighten the running backstays several clicks.

You're crazy, too inexperienced...

The silver and grey bird is hovering nearby, about 14 inches across. He swings away and returns to expose his bright silver grey belly and a beak that is twice as long as his head.

He is stalking something. He is far from land for such a small bird.

Independence Day arrived hot and blustery with a silver sun that reached its peak in a mottled sky within 21 seconds of my prediction. This was an encouraging sign that I could now estimate the arrival of noon by reckoning where I was in the ocean.

A pair of sights later in the afternoon, adjusted backwards in time, confirmed Feo's midday position at 21 degrees 58 minutes North, 151 degrees 42 minutes West. She had logged 158 miles in 24 hours, a creditable pace in a stiff wind with everything flying. We were still 200 miles from Hilo, but the tempo quickened amid fears about vessel traffic, the prospect of violent rainstorms and the uncertain time of landfall. The real danger lay here all along.

Aiming northeast of Hilo, (not believing I would find it on the first try) I was prepared to fulfill the prediction that no matter when you leave, everyone arrives in Hawaii in the dark. I thought this was amusing when one of the Transpac racers joked about it at their meeting, but it didn't seem quite so funny now.

Hilo Bay is eight miles wide, with tall bluffs along the western edge and low-lying black lava formations to the east. The harbor lies in the crook of a bay that is shaped like the figure 7. Open at the bottom, the long side runs north-south, the crook at the far end lying east-west.

Eight miles north of the city, at the near end of the 7, Peepeekio Light would appear first. It is 147 feet high and darkens for four seconds between white flashes. The Pilot said it can be seen in clear weather and calm water at a distance of 14 miles.

Six miles further south on the bluffs stands Paukaa Point Light, a 145-foot green flasher. Then a mile or so beyond is an inactive sugar mill with a large stack and unlit stone abutment. A mile across open water from that is the end of the breakwater, which protects another green lighted buoy in the harbor. I did not know what else might lie onshore, besides a 24-hour revolving airport beacon behind Hilo itself, marked on Charley's chart. Automobile headlights coming downhill could be expected to flash like beacons at perplexing intervals.

According to Charley's rendering, I could sail south along the bluff until a point opposite the sugar mill before turning inside the breakwater. A fleet of fishing boats would be working the outer reaches of the Bay.

Keep a sharp lookout.

The trade winds would also drive a sizable swell down the mouth of the Bay. Beyond the breakwater I would find a square mile of three-fathom holding ground in the lee of a small island but I was afraid that if I got too far downwind in this cul-de-sac I might be pinned by rain squalls against the western shore and have no way out. With the windlass frozen I could not drop anchor easily — and maybe not at all if the conditions were too rough.

Who knew what hazards Charley might have omitted from his drawing? I did not know, mostly at night, with distances so hard to judge. I wanted an infrared military scope capable of spotting a man's face in the dark at five miles, marked by the heat of his blood.

A voice kept saying, *prepare, prepare,* and I buzzed from one activity to another.

Take out the chain, check the connections.

Pulling the chain up from the hold onto the deck was equal to about 125 chin-ups. The chain sprawled across the deck and threatened to snake overboard as Feo's bow rushed on downwind, so I would have to coil it and tie it down.

Reread everything Chapman says about anchoring in shallows around coral reefs.

Our anchor line should be 8-10 times the depth of the water. I pulled out 150-feet of nylon anchor line, coiled and tied it on deck with the chain, just in case. Charley warned against closing on shore nearer than two miles.

Never go into a Hawaiian harbor at night.

From his drawings I tried to picture the landfall. The relative colors of tropical water would be alien. Brighter green water in daytime indicates shallows. I penciled the positions of each light onto a single plotting sheet. I might have to be very close to see them, even Point Kumukahi, the 165-foot flasher marking the easternmost end of the island, nineteen miles southeast of Hilo.

Around Kumukahi lay several thousand miles of ocean, all downwind. What if I rounded that last corner of land to the east, and sailed half a night before discovering the error?

I was finding it more and more difficult to shoot the sun with crossing seas that rushed underneath from an acute angle behind us. The noon sun had been moving more directly overhead as we approached the equator, 88 degrees at the last noon sighting, and now began to reach its peak just to the north. Now the noon angle had to be calculated differently from the tables.

My late afternoon shot made no sense, and another one was even more incoherent. The two together failed to produce a line of position.

Was it the low angle of the sun, something awry in the sextant? Was it the lower latitudes in which we now found ourselves?

I sweated profusely in the thick cabin humidity, my mind too vague to get clear answers from the books. I felt my confidence unraveling now, just when I was supposed to have it all down pat. I made myself stop, cook dinner, eat, and rest, even if I could not sleep. I had learned to take care of myself this way, sometimes pausing to handle my good-luck charm, the circles that saved the fisherman when his mates were lost. I reached for an opera tape, only to discover the cassette/radio had worked itself up against the cabin wall, turned itself on, and had run the batteries dead. The last set of batteries was being saved to listen for Hawaiian music from a Hilo radio station — if there was one anywhere around.

On a course just a degree west of south I found myself enrapt by the night sky as the waxing moon chased us. The wind picked up stiffly and I stood on deck in a sea of star-swept phosphorescence, with rollers climbing to twice my height, cauldrons of brilliant black gamboling in pursuit as Feo left her smoldering trail of pale green flame.

I piled cushions on the aft hatch, bundled myself against the wind and lay with my back against the mizzen mast to watch Feo's mainmast and spreaders tilt against the sky. Like a diaphanous curtain drawn over the opening to another universe, the Aurora Borealis appeared as the map of Italy, calf and boot outlined by pins of white steel in a black well.

Never had I seen so many points of light nor darkness as pure as the one rising here, without land or lights or any sign of civilization. I might have been sailing across some huge eye, an earthly upward gaze at the heavens on which we found ourselves a tiny speck. These southern stars and constellations were beginning to descend on me. Or was I rising among them?

What was this zigzag line of stars that led us south? Norma, Scorpius, Ophiuchus...

Ancient navigators had picked their way along these points, but I had no desire to capture them in the sextant. I traced their outlines and marveled at the billions of years it took these light impulses to reach this place as I tried to drink them all in.

Looking back north at Polaris I could see The Big Dipper tipped down to the west, handle aloft, ready to pour its dark contents onto the horizon. East of Polaris hung Cassiopeia, a chair unsettled. There was Andromeda, stickman with a swelled trapezoid for a head, with Hercules straight overhead like Fred Astaire in white tie and tails — my father's unrequited ambition as a ballroom dancer, debonair on bent knee. Viewed in reverse to the south, the same figure might be seen as an odd swastika, deranged by centrifugal force.

Feo's course now seemed to fall along the path between Hercules and the Corona Borealis, through the narrow aperture between two faint stars and into a widening V of blackness, beyond two figures called Bootes and little Draco.

———

Lower down crouched Scorpius, beginning his decline to the horizon with his thin back arched and thick tail cocked, the brilliant Antares at the center of his head. There was Cygnus, like an elongated cross straight above, with Pegasus in pursuit of Andromeda to the east. Scarcely more than names in dimly recollected mythology, they now seemed to prefigure history itself, as points of wonder in the void. They bound all humankind and cultures together in the desire to recognize patterns and the need to find meaning, to connect dots and give name to things vaguely perceived, and to address the eternal curiosity:

How might this have begun? And what was our place in it, our own meaning?

I had read the Bible in school but still did not believe that any all-powerful God had ordained it. I had never bought the story about a chosen people rewarded by God at the expense of others. It would be out of character for a loving and righteous God to pick one people over others, it seemed to me, no matter what they called themselves. Nor did I believe that science had found final answers in a Black Hole or a Big Bang. Some infinitely powerful explosion of non-matter had created what hung above me now? And what was there before that?

Explanations of religion and science rang empty to me in the end. "Humans are like a carburetor trying to explain General Motors," an uncle of mine once said.

Let go of the compulsion to figure it out. These heavens were as mysterious as I might ever find the strength to admit.

"Imagine," said Professor Bill White. He was sitting stiffly in a garden at the Harvard Business School where he had taught capital market theory for two decades. He had just discovered he was dying of leukemia, and undergone his first chemotherapy,

but he would keep on teaching until the last. I was among many who felt blessed to know this great teacher. He seemed to grow more devout as his time approached.

"Imagine that God put you on earth to find yourself in spirit," he said.

We had stopped talking about the role of banks in wealth creation and the nature of America's economy, the subject of my fellowship for that year. He handed me his notes from a Divinity School lecture that had moved him deeply.

"Everyone seeks communion, intimacy, and ecstasy," he said. "Particularly ecstasy, which is missing from so many lives. And fruitfulness, which we only bring forth from openness and intimacy."

These stars seen from any other planetary angle would make constellations of another kind. So much depended on place and time, and the angle they afforded — your point of view. And we felt compelled to find patterns, or a formula, without which there seemed to be no meaning. That was the Western mind at work.

Named by astronomers or still anonymous, the stars mocked my musings with their distance and their unfathomable being.

Find meaning in the disorder, and faith within that.

T he next day found us 90 miles out and closing fast amid jostling potato heads and sudden rain squalls that left a marching line of rainbows behind us.

I stood on the companionway steps, half out the hatch, facing the morning sun. A flock of white birds dove past in pursuit of the flying fish. Seas that unnerved me two weeks ago passed like old acquaintances. I was thinking *I can locate myself, set a course, hold it, and find myself noon to noon.*

The Gunning vane, my silent and steadfast crewman, had been steering his usual steady course, but I kept tinkering with it and recording the compass reading each time, to track the average.

Keep Feo as close to 210 degrees as possible. Paukaa is that way.

Everything would converge, the navigation and preparation, my fatigue and penchant for error. The big seas were now coming from the port quarter, and more from the northeast than I expected.

Snatch some sleep in the daylight.

A few miles off-course at this angle and we would miss Kumukahi. There was no point reassembling the water pump for a dead engine. I stowed all the toolboxes and cleaned up again.

Eat well through the day.

I missed the estimated time of noon by four and a half minutes. The sight reduction did not fall even close to my dead reckoning, 30 miles east.

If the noon shot were right, we were now just 60 miles away from Hilo, 10 hours from shore.

Where did this 30-mile error come from?

Hoping to figure out the answer, I accepted the noon sight and used another sun shot from three hours later in the afternoon, which produced a position 46 miles from Paukaa.

No, I could not have come so far in a day. I assumed a more southerly course since the day before and conjured up a third position, further from Hilo.

Now I had three positions on the plotting sheet — the noon shot, the daily reckoning and my second-guessing. They spanned 40 miles. Each required a significantly different course to find the mouth of Hilo.

I took a break from my deepening confusion to make a large pot of stew, enough food to get me through the night and into the next day. I felt nauseated. Maybe at two miles offshore you can hit a night reef before you hear surf. But nothing on the big ocean chart suggests outlying shoals.

With three alternative positions, I had to rely on new calculations where nothing was known for sure. I grew furious at the instruments and charts, which overwhelmed my small table but refused to divulge useful answers. The island is 72 miles wide as I face it. What if I have been making the same mistake over and over in plotting noon positions?

Are you fucking stupid?

I drew all three courses that could bring me to Peepeekio on the west, or Kumukahi on the east, or to Hilo's mouth between. The plotting sheet now resembled an oriental fan, a thicket of my own creation. I either was or wasn't where I thought I might or might not be. One of these courses might be right.

But which one? If only a light would appear.

I begin searching for a long cabin cushion that seemed to be nowhere on the boat, not in any of the lockers or storage bins. *Where the fuck had it gone?* I need it in the starboard berth so I can rest.

I suddenly realized there is no such cushion, and there never was.

I am losing it.

I could not stay away from the chart with its lunatic cross hatchings. I could not stay off the deck where the afternoon haze hung to the southwest like flat silver corrugation.

Surely I should see Mauna Kea's peak at 13,796 feet or Mauna Loa's at 13,677. The old-timer said you could see the conical land masses rising through the cloud line if you knew what to look for. By night, I should see airplanes descending into Hilo.

Alternative position C was a good compromise, betting my course and distance were correct but the sextant shot was faulty somehow. The mirrors must be out of whack after all this use. These tiny screw fittings would re-angle the glass.

Why are you doing this now? Maybe you're putting new error in, not taking old error out.

The question was barely formed when the little screw turned. Too late. The drawing in the manual showed how to realign the horizon.

Another sun line and the latitude produced a new fix within 50 miles of Hilo. Position A had been right after all.

I changed course again. (It did not occur to me until much later that one knot of trade wind-driven surface current was worth 24 miles of lateral movement per day. I should have seen at this moment that the noon sight was accurate after all. The set and drift of ocean and wind were actually forcing me 20-30 miles west every 10 hours.)

The clouds seem to be stacking ahead and assumed the shape of the island. Maybe the radio could find something. I balanced it on the forward hatch and aimed the antenna at the cluster of clouds.

Ukulele music!!!

An ad for Ralph's Burgers in Hilo blared and the antenna pointed to an AM station slightly off the port bow, where my last position suggested Hilo should be.

I jammed the tape of *La Boheme* into the cassette and blasted it out over the water. Rudolpho declared his love to Mimi as they descended the stairs at the end of Act I to join friends in the village. The sun hit the horizon in a band of lily orange, but for all the sudden rush of light and music I felt uneasy.

Somehow, much more lay ahead.

T he ocean changed now in the unspoken presence of others, coming or going from Hilo and the western reaches of the islands. I felt them out there, cable-drawn barges behind ocean tugs, towed on cable hawsers a quarter-mile long that could cut you down in the fog. Sail between the tug and the barge on the illusion that they are unrelated boats and that will be your undoing, my father had warned me years ago. We were watching a pair of over-and-under lights cross our path in Block Island Sound when I was 12 or so, and he demonstrated how easily the lights could be mistaken for something on shore.

"That could be your last mistake," he said.

Tugs and trawlers on short hops from Honolulu to Hilo would steam in and out in the rain and fog and darkness, hour by hour, along with inbound freighters.

Another hour passed. Feo lisped along. The wind made up out of the northeast and my eyes strained into the darkness. Rain squalls rose quickly, sizzled on approach as the wind lifted and swept by, a swift, rising sound that drove Feo's rail under. The sky would clear for flickers of starlight before another squall came down to hiss and drum its way across the deck. I could not see beyond Feo's deck in any direction.

A red light blinked suddenly straight ahead, a ship's port light. It turned green now, a starboard light, coming straight on!

Then it disappeared.

The vane was holding Feo to the Paukaa course. I kept eating stew and drinking coffee to stay awake. The green light reappeared ahead. This time it was steady.

It could not be Paukaa, and not a ship, as it was green only, and fixed. Could it be the light at the head of the harbor shown on Charley's chart? But how far must that be? If I can see that, shouldn't I see Peepeekio and Paukaa by now? Maybe fog is hanging in a bank above them.

In another half hour, off to the left of the green beacon, an intermittent shaft of light moved in a semicircle, like a windshield wiper repeatedly waving left to right. Again. And again.

That's the aero beacon. The green light is the head of the harbor.

Surely there was enough power in the batteries to put out a quick call. The red transmission light signaled weakly as I spoke:

"Feo calling Coast Guard Hilo. Coast Guard Hilo, come in, please. Over.."

"This is Coast Guard Hilo, come in Feo. Over," said the voice of a teenager.

"This is Feo, 21 days out of San Francisco, single-handed. My engine is down, got no power for lights. I've got no chart of Hilo. I'm in the mouth of Hilo Bay somewhere. Can you direct me, over?"

"You want a tow? Over."

"No, thanks, no tow necessary. Just need to find a safe zone 'til morning. Over."

"U.S. Coast Guard is not authorized to give navigational aid. Over."

Why have I been paying taxes?

"Visibility poor here. Cannot identify traffic zones, hazards. Can you locate me on radar? Confirm my position, over?"

"Negative, Feo. Not authorized to give navigational aid, over."

Another rain squall spattered past. I did not want to be down below in the cabin if a fishing trawler should happen to plow into a sailing vessel with no lights at the mouth of Hawaii's second-busiest port.

"Feo standing off 'til morning, over."

"Acknowledged. U.S. Coast Guard Hilo clear. Over and out."

Back on deck I stared ahead at the light. To the east and south would be Blonde Reef. If I turned Feo that way I would cross the wide mouth of Hilo Bay and the path of every inbound or outbound vessel. In the rain squalls in the dark I would not hear or see anyone until they were upon me.

I could either bear off to sail downwind along the coast, or I could try to beat back northeast. I should not get too far offshore. I went aft to take the vane blade off, and jibed, and Feo came around swiftly with a bang. Her bowsprit leaped and plunged as I cinched the sails tighter on the wind. Coming downwind for hours as the swells built I hadn't realized how hard the wind was blowing and how steep these seas had become. The anchor buried itself violently in green water and I eased away from the wind a few degrees to quiet her motion. I did not want to expose Feo alone to whatever was out here, but I could barely stand. I went below into the thrashing sound of steel against these northeast driven swells.

Emily's last message fell on this afternoon, here on the brink.

Dear dad, How are you? I am fine. How's the weather? How was the trip? I love you. P.S. Please write back. Love, Emily.

It was 8 p.m. for her in Stockton, and it had been three weeks since we'd spoken, an eternity for a six-year-old.

"Hey, what about this?" cried the Stick Man, pointing to a flock of something that might have been the letter T on its side.

Are they schools when they swim
and flocks when they fly?
The fish don't answer
As they fly by...

I wolfed down the remaining stew from the day before, and decided to sleep, just for an hour or so. After all, I was practically there.

In a recurrent nightmare, I face a final exam with the knowledge that I have not attended the lectures or read any of the books. The climax of this dream is always the same — a moment of anxious desperation and futility. I am trapped and helpless.

I woke from this dream in humid light to hear Feo thrashing laboriously ahead.

Oh my God we are sailing away from Hilo.

I burst up out of the hatch to face white-tipped combers from the northeast, and to sense land looming somewhere off to port, where Kauiki Head on the eastern tip of Maui must be. I saw the compass heading at 350 and realized I had slept for nearly seven hours. So Feo would have covered between thirty and forty miles, high into the Alenuihaha Channel where the trade winds funnel between Maui and Hawaii. Little chance of a sun shot in this overcast, perhaps not all day.

Feo fought her way around in the frothy grey-green seas to begin a long beat back through the impenetrable grey, riddled with more rain squalls. I lost any sense of progress, staring for land ahead, scanning the vague horizon every few minutes. The radio report kept repeating the same weather conditions: trade winds of 20-30 knots along the north shore of Hawaii, heavy rain intermittent in Hilo Bay. No hurricanes or tropical storm warnings.

At times in mid-ocean I had been disoriented, but now I felt dangerously lost, as much from fatigue as uncertainty among the islands. The rain turned steady in the late afternoon and held on. As night approached the wind fell and the rain wisped away.

Before long, Feo was just drifting.

———————

Something rose up ahead, not sky but something solid, with pinpoints of light here and there. They might be boats. Something flashed and disappeared.

Fog descended, then wind rose to blow it away. Dead calm returned.

Feo fell into a mysterious creaking, rolling with a motion I had never felt before. It was strangely grey-black here, colors of volcanic rock and ash. The wind came back, rain with it. Fog swept over us.

I listened like a fanatic for any leaping noise that might arise. An engine rose and faded vaguely in the direction of Hilo. Voices emanated from shore. I was starved for sleep but pricked awake by listening and these sudden flighty sounds, and waiting, waiting in this opaque, not-quite darkness of steely fog and rain. The rain let up as real darkness began to edge downward.

A ghostly shoreline bent away to the south and east, a pale glow of rim line light that must be Hilo glowing in the dark. Land straight ahead, houses along a roadway, a mountain road somewhere because headlights unwound in a flickering downward corkscrew.

In dead calm again the rudder made a hunkering noise as Feo drifted toward the shoreline. People came and went in the woods. Houses overhung the water. Dark rocks rose to a thin line of trees. I could see vegetation in somber patches against the fields above, a single house tucked up into a gorge. Any closer and we would strike the edge of their lawn.

With the engine working we would be just a few hours from the city. Yeah, and if my aunt were a man she'd be my uncle. The shore moves past, closer. Feo might be drifting over the ground toward the rocks, or stationary.

If I have to drop the anchor suddenly to keep us off the reefs, I'd better get the chain onto the deck in readiness. The clanking ricocheted off toward the shore and returned like a second chain uncoiling nearby.

In British Columbia the ferry captains used to shout toward shore and measure the time it took their voices to come back, and they could come right up the channel to the wharf like that in dense fog. Dad is standing beside me on the Saltspring Island ferry as we approach Ganges for my first time, when all the brothers gathered to celebrate our grandparents' 50th anniversary.

"Try it," he said. "See how long it takes before your voice comes back." I let loose a faint "hello!" and listened to it disappear into the mist.

Wind rose faintly from the southeast now and curled along the embankment. Feo slipped toward open water as the dark descended across Hilo Bay.

The freighter traffic must surely come.

I hunched in the cockpit with every nerve ending alive. Vaporous rains returned with wind from the south and Feo stole eastward. The rain stopped and we stopped. A fishing boat hung nearby, electric eyes watching without blinking, motionless, and then crawled off toward Hilo. The sound of the motor was here now and gone, resonating back along a shoreline. My loaded flare-gun lay in wait in the cockpit.

❀

I woke with the sun rising. Feo had been creeping east between rain showers but now was making about four knots northeast as the wind shifted north out of a shapeless sky. I turned her back southeast. I needed a shot at the sun.

———

An attack of cottonmouth cemented my lips. I was running low on non-alcohol beer and was not sure how long it had been since my last good meal — curried chicken and wild rice with mixed vegetables, dried currents and cashews. The canned chicken and wild rice were gone. I had just stabbed myself with the sharp end of the navigating compass, my first self-inflicted wound in 22 days. A reminder.

Be careful on deck.

❀

The sky broke into geographical fragments of blue and the flat white horizon began to dissolve at last. The hint of a huge dark triangle materialized faintly above a rumpled cloud-line to the south.

Hawaii!

So long elusive, she could not have emerged from the mist or descended from the clouds with more perfect stealth and grace than she now presented herself. Featureless mound coming clear, the Big Island rose from the water like a conjurer's trick, the answer to all my fierce machinations, a nearly perfect natural pyramid suggesting untold immensity beneath. The ocean and elements that had put me through a crucible of anxiety and inexperience offered her now after 2,200 miles — if I could just make my way ashore.

Sunlight descended over that distant pyramid as Feo advanced on an English green patchwork countryside above charred bluffs. Pale land dotted with trees ran up an incline across barren hills into dark brown volcanic highlands. The blunt peak vanished again into the clouds, one mountain where there should be two. Its ridges descended equally east and west to distant rapier points at the water's edge.

Where were the twin giants of Mauna Kea and Mauna Loa, waiting to usher us in?

T he tall cinder cones that were to mark Hilo's eastern edge and Kumukahi still further east were nowhere to be seen. My chart showed Hawaii's northern face, from Hilo's western lip onward, nearly barren of navigational aids — nothing from Peepeekio for another 13 miles west to Laupahoehoe, a black and white marker on a black rock. Through the binoculars I could see only intermittent red and white dots across fields and roads that wound like tiny threads through the grass. No coves or harbors or identifiable markings along the shore either way. The Rolling Stones blared from Oahu to the northwest. A Maui station beamed Beach Boys without commercial interruption. No signal to identify Hilo as I spun the radio direction-finder back and forth.

Feo approached the land at an acute angle within several miles of sheer rock off to starboard until I could make out windows in a house on the bluff above. The sky had cleared and occasional whitecaps broke. I searched for some hint that the city lay ahead to the east around that next point. The water lightened to dark jade. Forced north by the angle of the wind, I took Feo about.

The sun was high and hot and I was soon singing and talking aloud to myself in a daze of pleasure and fatigue, the deck metal hot to my skin. The downhaul for the boom had unwound itself during the night and I was in the middle of fixing it —

My watch! It was already 22:20 hours in Greenwich! Too close to noon!

I cursed myself below, grabbed the sextant and came up shooting almost straight overhead at the huge and torrid sun.

87 degrees, 44 minutes. Then 87 degrees, 29 minutes. Then 87:16.

The sun was already descending.

"God damn you stupid idiot!! How could you miss *this* noon sight of all the fucking noon sights to miss? You *fucking* moron."

Much later, I would realize: I should have calmed myself, this fury was no friend. I should have gone below to plot a line of position and ask myself: "Okay, where must you be? East of Hilo, or west?'

If west, we had to beat further offshore and claw our way back upwind. That would be torture. If east, Hilo was a quick downwind sail, three hours at the most.

But plotting the sun's angle just at that moment meant wrestling with numbers down below on a sweaty tropical afternoon. Poised on Hawaii's exotic threshold, in a state mixing exhaustion and complacency — we were, after all, nearly there — I instead took the easy way and gave Feo her head. She dove across the stark blue and white-capped water with a rush, heading sharply offshore. With the hot breath of the trade wind rising, the island floated elegantly in primitive pale green splendor, just the tip of her mysteries revealed. Something in me did not care what I needed to know just then. I was only too happy to release Feo down that ribbon of rising plain and desert slope.

But where exactly am I? Is this the right way to go?

I ignored that voice and like an exhausted horse that has been turned at last toward the barn, Feo foamed happily on past a bright yellow swatch of a farmhouse planted amid dark furrows and alfalfa green fields. An upland barn gushed steam or smoke into a widening white ribbon that joined the clouds downwind. The water's edge was all sheer bluff of volcanic rock, red tints among the earth jewels in a strange land.

Hilo was very likely around that next bend.

I put on the baggy white cotton shirt that my sister had made for me and sat against the bleached hull of the dinghy in a patch of shade. The backs of these downwind seas took on the sheen of taut blue bodices in collision and I thought maybe I had never seen a more beautiful scene in all my life.

I woke several times with a start. The mountain horizon began to subdivide into a second line of descent, another distant mountain. I could not make out either Mauna Loa or Kea and I began to feel slightly sick to my stomach, unsure whether Hilo lay ahead or behind.

A distant bluff turned and ran back inland as a blackened fissure south into the island. Maybe I was about to come around the short end of the '7' into Hilo Bay. This did not look like an opening eight miles across, let alone a few miles deep. Blonde Reef should appear at any moment beyond the next dark point of stone.

Suddenly visible was a deep gash of rock on the far side, similar to an inlet on Charley's rendering of west Hilo Bay, but with no mill. The water color was getting lighter, toward green but still blue, around the 20-fathom line. I spotted a tug and barge crossing several miles to the north, heading east, a deadly tow cable between.

Why would they be going in that direction unless Hilo is also that way?

T he slash of bluffs led to a deep gouge in the coastal wall. Dark cliffs at a dead-end closed off any avenue of hope, however foolish, that a major harbor lay in there. No Hilo here.

Blame our blind desire that things be what they are not.

The sun fell into dark clouds above the island as I went forward to repack the anchor chain below, then set the smaller jib and reef the main. I would have to beat a long way offshore to get back upwind to where Hilo must be.

How long can I keep this up without being run down?

I winched Feo as close to the wind as she would sail with any speed. After the 21st day, I was afraid Emily would become afraid of what might have happened to me.

I am not in control.

Maybe the point was to come to this point.

I cut up an onion into a pot of leftover beans, added a can of spaghetti sauce and noodles enough to last for two days. Braced at the stove, stirring and sweating and spattered with spaghetti sauce and mumbling to myself, I tried to work my way to a sure sense of where I must be.

Hawaii has one northern face. You are heading north from some point along its western third. Forget that you got so close and then turned away from Hilo like an idiot. What matters now is getting far enough northeast to fetch it on return. You almost did it before, and you can do it again. Make sure you get a noon shot tomorrow.

I caught myself wishing for the impossible. I wanted the trade winds to shift around suddenly to come out of the north, which had never happened in my lifetime or that of any mariner throughout history. I wanted clear, gentle nights and a calm fix on Hilo's shore lights.

With the island falling away behind and the sails set for the night, Feo hobby-horsed violently into the oncoming seas. The cabin air felt like sweat itself. I forced myself to eat, change into a clean T-shirt and shorts.

A prickly, atmospheric sensation crept over me. Apprehension unfolded along my skin like animal awareness:

Someone or something is here.

On deck earlier, I had imagined another presence that at first I took to be my own, disembodied from me. Now that someone or something was below with me. This was not an illusion but a palpable sense of some other. What was this, and why was it happening now?

I went on deck to cool off.

Something is here with me.

A forest fire burned in the western ocean. Soot and smoke billowed in from the northeast. Pugnacious, dirty clouds fed my confusion, fulminating mountain ranges to the north where there were none. Maui's Haleakala peak must be further west.

I looked back south at the fading profile of Hawaii, chasms in volcanic bluffs where a line of giant chimpanzee heads stared as I came to the certain knowledge I had been sailing in the wrong direction all afternoon. They watched me retreat offshore.

It is pointless to blame yourself.

My friend from Boston came to search for me in a remote village. I was talking to a cluster of townspeople about how far along the main street a painted wooden sign should hang. I did not know what the sign would say. I am not well known in what is obviously an enclave of formerly married men. My friend has the look of a big country farm girl, short brown hair in an athletic cut, a wide, open attractive face, large breasts on a powerful build. She has the shoulders of a competitive swimmer and strong hands that have evidently worked the earth. She waits nearby for a while, but grows restless that I am deep in conversation with the owner of the boat yard where Feo has just been refitted. She drifts away to find a room of her own somewhere in the town, leaving behind a note that says:

"You do not have to give up your child just because you are not the mother. She is half yours, too."

Something in her words woke me. This dream was too real to shake off easily. I went on deck to check the wind and scan for freighters, then hiked over the railing astern to relieve myself, since I had given up using the head below or even a bucket in the cockpit. Feo seethed into a squall of small-caliber bullets that hit sharply and then thickened into molten drops. Back inboard, I stripped off my harness and T-shirt and stood naked in the cockpit, feeling the drumbeat of warm rain on me and Feo all at once.

This night was not a single darkness but was divided among black ocean and smoke of an onrushing storm, faint patches of darker night I now recognized as imminent cloudbursts. Rain coursed down my back and legs. I rubbed it into every pore and crevice and felt my skin dissolve into the wind.

The light of dawn was beginning to edge over the horizon when I climbed back down below and spread a dry sheet on the bunk. I was acutely uncomfortable. Why couldn't I relax, naked and alone in that darkness? My body felt it belonged to someone else, out of my control.

Emily and I were leaving the boat yard together after the mast came out and she was about to turn six. She climbed into the car in the front seat beside me.

"Dad, why can't you and Mom be together? That's what I don't get."

"Darling, if I could give you what you want, I would," I said. "But I can't. After a few years maybe you will understand better. I can't make things the way you want them to be, or the way I want them to be."

She paused to absorb this. "Neither can I." Then she started to cry, and so did I. We sat in the car together like that until our tears ran out, and then it was time for me to drive her back into the Valley to meet her mother.

Half-wrapped in the damp sheet now I thought: You begin to wear shoes before you realize they do not fit. Eventually you realize you will be crippled over time if you don't get out of them.

Something was in the way. Her mother and I somehow never learned to forgive and to comfort each other in the hardest times. At least I didn't. Anyone can be good in the good times. We did not care enough, or simply did not know how. Something.

How could I help my daughter understand what I could barely grasp myself: it was right to end the marriage, and wrong, too. Vows broken, the promise of family ruptured for a growing child.

I would try to make up for what I had taken away in what I could still give.

Feo slogged ahead inches at a time in a gale about 50 miles offshore. Her bow pounded the oncoming seas and she trembled at forces let loose through her mast. An alien creak emanated from the forward bulkhead, where the mast support ran from deck to hull. The motion of the water had changed again, forest fire smoke everywhere east and north. The wind gusted furiously through the shrouds and I wondered whether the rigging could endure.

CRASH!

Green water slammed the anchor into the bowsprit as the bow plunged into a wave. Feo stalled, held in irons by the vane pressing her upwind and the seas forcing her off. The forest fire leapt up in the east, orange mixed with rose and streaked with black. I turned her back southeast, too focused on Hilo to realize then that we could have easily turned and run around the north side of Maui to Kahului Harbor, a simple reach by nightfall. But my mind was now shut to the very alternatives it had considered two days before when my mind was less riddled by fatigue.

Sailing fast, I tried to take a shot of the moon but couldn't fix the horizon amid these charging mounds and wallowing pits. The clouds broke open now and again. The waves hung tall and unpredictable. I waited for more than an hour after breakfast, lodged in the companionway until I got one sun shot. Its line made no sense. I caught another an hour later. Afraid to miss noon I started shooting too early, and took 36 sights in 52 minutes. At last I had a position, 65 miles north and just east of Peepeekio. Still more than 14 hours of hard sailing from Hilo.

The wind and seas and current kept pushing us west of our course, but just how much ground we lost each hour I could not calculate. When I brought the morning sun line up to the noon latitude, the intersection put us 40 miles east of the noon position, hugely in conflict with my dead reckoning. I did not know which position to throw out, or what course to set. The options ranged from 166 to 203 degrees — a frightening spread either side of due south. I hedged toward the middle with a sense that this might not be a good solution.

Just as I came out of the cabin to scan for the vague mountain again something large whispered off my right shoulder: an eight-foot pole on a floating yellow steel ball at least six feet in diameter. Feo had missed one of the state's fish-aggregating buoys by a quarter of a boat-length

I took a photo of it as it fell behind, and caught sight of a grey military profile drawing closer, deceptively fast. I waited until it was about a half-mile mile away.

"Feo to unidentified military vessel about 40 miles north Hilo. Feo to Navy cruiser, come in please, over..."

The radio crackled faintly.

———

"San Francisco to Hilo, inbound, want to confirm my position, over."

Maybe this cruiser was out here on a military dragnet for smugglers. Maybe the DEA didn't want to chat.

The radio buzzed.

"Feo, this is U.S. Coast Guard Honolulu responding. Feo, come in. Please identify, over..."

"Feo, 47-foot ketch, inbound Hilo from San Francisco, over..."

"Did you just ask for assistance, over?"

"No. Well, sort of. I spoke to Coast Guard Hilo two nights ago. Over."

"You called around midnight, Feo? You requested tow, over?"

"No. Spoke to Hilo the night before. Did not request tow, over.."

"You called last night, over?"

"Negative. Negative. Not last night. Over."

"Someone else called last night, Feo? Inbound yacht requesting assistance. Not you, over?"

My radio light was winking faintly and I was sure he would not hear whatever I had to say.

"Not me. Feo signing off," I said, and clicked off.

Outside, the cruiser faded to the northeast and disappeared into oncoming rain clouds.

The sky opened up briefly in mid-afternoon and I got three sights in three minutes. The first two gave me a pair of lines so close I treated them as one. Peepeekio was now 41 miles away. Another eight or nine hours at this pace, on a course of 150 degrees, would bring me into the center of Hilo Bay — in the dead of night, once again.

Feo worked hard to make progress again toward the elusive green light. Rain squalls slashed in from the northeast and closed the night down like a march of black veils, letting up suddenly to leave eerie silences between them. I felt the ocean wind divide around the island mountain and sweep across us in an accelerating arc. Random shore lights marked a flat constellation across the plane of dark water, yellow stars and vague planets that winked in an irregular line and etched a trail left and right, near to far. They took on a motion their own, approaching and receding, and promontory became inlet by magic.

In squall after squall a light blinked that might have been Paukaa. Another blinked downwind, perhaps Peepeekio. Neither was visible long enough to identify. The lights loomed as if the constellation had taken a giant step forward. Then another set arose, a hillside or mountain ridge or random roadway, a river path along a curve of land that might or might not be there.

An elongated channel beckoned, but nothing like it showed on the chart. Another flashing light appeared, maybe Peepeekio, but it blinked at the wrong intervals and suddenly it did not blink at all. It must be too low or cut off by rollers rising in between us.

In several hours of driving across to the island, fighting north a few miles and then turning to come back again, Feo was unable to work her way upwind and I felt powerless to help. Charcoal clouds billowed upwards, forbidding apparitions of the night that seemed to drag on to no end.

The seas had built steeply as we approached a cluster of bright lights like an old sawmill I remembered in the woods in Massachusetts near home, and I went forward to set the smaller jib, to ease the strain on the rigging and improve our angle of sailing. The rain pelted in amber light, the half-moon visible through an aperture of cloud, and Feo's bowsprit leaped and dived like a carnival ride gone amok. Weightless in the plummeting downward rush toward the next trough, I crouched in the bowsprit to take the jib off before the thickest, wind-laden clouds arrived.

I am suddenly 14 again in Candida's bow pulpit, fighting to get her jib down before the worst of an approaching thunder squall catches up to us near Cape Porpoise. My father is gripping the tiller with his left hand, he is grinning through the rain and with his right hand gesturing to say, "Stay low to the deck and keep one hand for yourself." The gust has blown his hood back, his face is all bright shining forehead and bushy eyebrows and dark moustache and brilliant, wide-open grin. He is depending on me to get this thing done quickly and delighting to see me unafraid. I have seen this look of expectant joy cross his face skiing, or dancing with my mother or sister, or watching my older brother on stage, but this one puts me squarely at its center. Now he is crouched in Feo's cockpit as if no time has passed between us, looking intensely along the deck at me, and his look penetrates me as none ever had before.

Something fell away from me in that instant and something else rushed into its place. Perhaps an understanding or love of sailing that he had meant to teach me, or had already taught me whether I realized it or not. Perhaps it was something passed on in my genes and cultivated from the first days of small sailboats in Penobscot Bay. This moment collected so much that I had left behind, or grown estranged from, and it all came in a rush with the warm amber light behind the rain and Feo pitching toward that circle of lights where the harbor lay. I was aware of being swept up in a vision of my father as original man, a boy grown to love his own boy, doing together what they both loved. I saw his love for his younger son with perfect clarity, unmixed with anger or brutality. I saw in it every gift he ever gave me or pride he had ever felt in me, everything he had hoped for me or wanted ever to explain, all now etched in his face aboard Feo. In that single look he reflected all the joy I felt in this bowsprit on my own, and he radiated it back as an effable moment of love and memory.

The rain and salt spray on my face were indistinguishable from sudden tears, swept back from my eyes by the wind. Could he feel this? Was something being transmitted across space and time? He might be sitting in his rocking chair on the porch in that Maine cottage now, the grey cottage shingles brought to a sheen by the rising sun on Eggemoggin Reach, his white hair like a flame against grey. Perhaps he had died just then, and I was being reborn in a vision of him as he had loved me privately, and to a depth I had never fully understood or appreciated. I was sure I had loved him before he taught me to hate him, though those emotions became so intertwined so early. For how much of my life had I been trapped between those two irreconcilable feelings?

———

Now a realization began to take shape even if I did not grasp it fully in that moment of storm-driven spray: I had come far enough to realize something at last. Wind-struck and enveloped by the night, I saw love more clearly — not just mine for my father but his for the boy who grew up believing deep in his heart that he must be guilty of something terrible to deserve the beatings. And I sensed, even if I did not yet know then, that without separating the cruelty from the love, and finding a way to forgive him, I could never hope to find my own way.

An apparition rose against the distant green shoreline. I was sprawled in the cockpit in the shadow of the wind, sweat-soaked in my yellow foul-weather gear on a tangle of uncoiled mainsail and jib and mizzen sheets. The staysail and large jib were stuffed in the cockpit with me, along with empty sail bags, winch handles, and binoculars — proof that I had given up stowing things away where they belonged.

Small cuts had appeared inside my index fingers on both hands. My right shoulder ached from some collision I couldn't recall. Running headlong at the shore, now less than two hours away, I dared not fall asleep in case I failed to turn Feo back from the dark bluffs or blundered into a reef. The light on Peepeekio had refused to reappear upwind. It must be around that next corner.

At about midnight I had spied what looked like a four-second flasher, but too far east. I tacked offshore again, and driven off repeatedly by those seas, struggled to hold Feo on an upwind course eastward on the way back in. Feo drove her rail deeper until the angle of the deck was too steep for safety. The seas would not let me turn her bow into the wind, which forced me to jibe off the wind again and again, losing precious ground each time. After a while, fantasy islands rose in the night off to the northeast where there could be nothing but open water. A freighter passed at close range inbound, if there was anything there at all.

Now dead ahead and thirty degrees up on that pale uprising green plain the apparition began to take on detail.

Pale, oddly shaped above.

Some kind of white plume, giant feather in a small cap.

Rock outcropping, a dark roof. Sand dunes beneath that hardened into yellow farmhouse walls.

Black squares, windows...

It's the yellow farmhouse.

Oh my God. That same yellow farmhouse. I see I have made absolutely no progress over the last three days and nights.

❀

Feo closed the gap slowly, now down drunkenly behind one after another wave that came from behind but broke left to right, driven by that wicked, steamy breeze along the island front. This wind blew a tiny howling into my ears from every angle, signaling it would give no quarter.

Tall whitecaps became powerful green combers that grew wider and taller as Feo fought to close on that rising shore. Wave tops blew off with a hiss into fine mist and turned the air to smoke. Dark clouds rolled in low from the northeast like a giant New England stone wall crowding us toward the land.

I pictured Feo on the surface of a boiling cauldron, trembling liquid landscape of another planet, truly arrived in some different state of being.

Feo drove on as the ugly truth of the farmhouse sank in. My hands and legs felt like deadweight and the island looming and wind rising and Feo going headlong toward shore forced me to consider: could I sustain this upwind battle? Should I heave-to in these channels, only to be blown downwind at several knots per hour? I could not keep doing what I had been doing and I could not do nothing.

The vane held Feo's bow well to windward of the farmhouse but the farmhouse did not shift in its relative position to us. That meant we were making as much leeway to the west as we were making headway south. Maybe I would have to give up on Hilo. Maybe I was too committed to it as a result of so much expended effort. Would giving up on Hilo be the right choice, or just quitting?

I went below to reheat the leftovers and ran the engine for several minutes to put a small charge into the batteries, but not enough to overheat it. The island loomed to a height that startled me. Vegetation broke into individual trees and shrubs. Against the wall-like shore a sail marched swiftly downwind, bright white triangle shooting the rapids of this rugged coast, her hull hidden by the seas between us.

The color of the water had begun to lighten. Just as we were about to lose sight of the farmhouse behind the cliffs, I jibed Feo back offshore and she went with a swoop, rolled wildly down between two crossing seas that pinned her sideways for a scary interval before they let her up.

There is no sailing into these waves. I can stay out here to be hammered or I can find another route.

Maui lay downwind and invisible with the promise of heavy winds and high seas around its southern tip. From here to Lanai was a straight open shot, aided all the way by ocean current — past the western tip of Hawaii through the Alenuihaha Channel, aided all the way by current. There was a good mark on the western tip of Kahoolawe, and then another 22 miles to Kaumalapau — 110 miles altogether. I studied the charts and pictured myself making the turn, finding the lighthouses through the night and entering Kaumalapau's — "a small bight in the most prominent gulch," according to the Coastal Pilot. My mind held the image and watched Feo make her entrance.

If I decided soon enough and let Feo fly, I would have this shoreline alongside all afternoon. Huge tanks on Upolu Point at the end of Hawaii. Kahoolawe impossible to miss. A well exposed flasher on Palaoa Point, southwest Lanai, in the night once again.

Trade winds gusting above 35 knots are not to be fought but joined. Instead of Hilo's rain squalls, expect sudden dead calms in the Kealaikahiki channel approaching Lanai, the Pilot warned. Errors will come more easily than ever.

I would welcome calm water now.

Feo thrashed along as I huddled in the cockpit to eat and keep watch, fighting a sense of dejection and failure. Hilo was beyond reach. If conditions could overpower me once, they could again. I had no energy to spend on regret. *Let go of everything behind, press on, keep going, now more than ever.* Emily was watching me now to see what I would do. I needed to get word to her that I had not disappeared.

"**U**S 909-690, this is sailing vessel Feo on Channel 16, calling Coast Guard Hilo, over."

"Coast Guard Hilo. Come in Feo."

The same young voice, without age or accent. "Feo. How do you spell that? Over."

"Frank-Echo-Oregon. Inbound San Francisco. Did I speak with you three nights ago? Over."

"Yes. Watch Officer Ainbinder here. Did you call again the next night, over?"

"No. Someone from Honolulu asked me that. Over."

"This is Honolulu. Over."

"I thought you were talking from Hilo. Over."

"Honolulu is Hilo, too. We're one station. Over."

No wonder he wouldn't advise me on the night approach. He was on Oahu!

"I'm overdue five days, want to check in. In case anyone is calling Coast Guard, trying to locate me. I was en route Honolulu but I lost my engine and lights. Over."

"No record of inquiry on you, Feo. We had another disabled sailboat seeking assistance. Was that you? Over."

"No, over."

"Not you? Over."

"No. Over."

"What's your position now, over?"

"Off Laupahoehoe. I couldn't make it upwind into Hilo after I got blown downwind. Over." I didn't need to tell him that I had fallen asleep to get myself to a point of no return.

"We have a San Diego yacht in trouble and we've got help en route to them. We can't get to you for another 15 hours. Do you want to stand by for a tow? Over."

"No. No tow. Can you call California? Tell my family I may be ashore in about two days? I've set a course for Lanai. Over."

"Government policy is that we cannot call out-of-state, over."

"Mr. Ainbinder, could you manage this as a personal favor? I'm almost a week late. They will take a collect call. A small child might worry about her father. Can you do that for me? Please? Over."

"Roger, Feo. Give me the number. I will see what I can do. Over and out."

"Thank you, Mr. Ainbinder." I gave him Emily's number and promised I would not forget.

※

Feo pivoted west and leaped ahead with the rushes of rolling ocean she had fought for days. Hawaii lay alongside like a fixture in the stream, mammoth stationary rock and carapace of the deep. Pale brown sugarcane climbed to barren slopes that vanished into flat white clouds. Towering shoreline rocks opened to long ravines, a cleft here in the bluff with a red-roofed village obscured by scrub evergreen at the far end. Waipio, said the chart. Thin roads cut into cane fields past isolated houses here and there. No sign of anyone moving.

Feo drove on past vacant gulches, antique idle trestles over beachfront cliffs, desolate concrete fixtures on the bluffs above, cylindrical grey storage tanks nesting in pairs. A few gorges reached back into the island around dark corners, creature-remains partly unburied by the sea, an angular volcanic skeleton ripped by surf, accessible to any small boat willing to risk itself on the rocks going in.

Maui held herself up to the north, Haleakala at 10,000 feet a grim volcanic peak in the haze 35 miles away, an island suggested but not defined.

Stay clear of Kauhola Point, a third of a mile of dangerous breakers, the Pilot said.

The wind whipped along the bluffs and accelerated as the island declined to the water, a tapered blade slicing the sky and sea to the west. Occasional Sentinel pines, stubbed and bent from centuries of prevailing wind, gestured west to Kahoolawe and Lanai, as yet invisible. At last the northwestern tip of Hawaii crawled out from under its own shroud, dwindled beyond the trio of tall round silos known as the Upolu Stacks, and tapered treeless to the water.

The seas were roiled shoulders crowding my cockpit chariot, hell-bent for the falling sun, ocean surf peaking but not quite breaking alongside that lifted and drove Feo with a forward-falling rush through this island breach that funneled the trade winds back into the open ocean.

"Pooshee! Pooshee!"

Four black backs exploded in curved unison off the stern as a quartet of porpoises startled me awake and frolicked with Feo through this maelstrom. We swept around the last low corner of the Big Island with Kahoolawe not yet visible beneath the bank of haze that I knew must mark something. To the southwest, the carved orange marble horizon of the Pacific extended all around, vague curvature of the planet and edge of the visible earth revealed, infinitely broad boulevard to the Equator and beyond to the Marshall and Mariana and Solomon Islands, Michel's adventures among the coral climates of undiscovered tribes, an expanse too vast to comprehend. The sun had swept through the noon spot and was arching midway down to that far line and shining back with a burning force of illumination, white-hot brand in a brilliant sky.

Whatever I had hoped to pull away from and leave behind, or what I had drawn away from in hopes of seeing more clearly from a greater distance, even as it all came along anyway — memories and fragments of memories and ruminations, connections that could not be broken or were yet to be made, all that I had set out to reach — seemed to converge here now, now that I was given up in exhaustion and awe and wonder to the conditions that embraced Feo as she sailed into that immense clearing. I felt myself utterly solitary and suspended, facing the edge of the world, needing only to hold this course through another night and catch a tiny hook of a harbor before she charged off that grand edge into oblivion.

Take a nap. Let the vane steer downwind in open water.

I went below for more food, the cabin riddled with sunspots through the portholes and a distant beehive hum in the hull, humming down through the shrouds.

The Presence is back.

Something corporeal — figment of the sun's heat? — was sitting still in the cockpit, a human form felt but unseen. I passed through it as I moved back and forth to adjust the vane and check the control lines for signs of chafe. I felt enveloped by it even though it seemed to be approximately my size. The sensation crawled upon me like the feeling when you know you are being followed but there is no one there to be seen. You learn only later that there really was someone behind you all the time.

Now the Presence was down below with me. It moved into the cockpit to tend the course while I searched the food locker for something to drink. It was there to help. I watched the sun cut through the portholes and streak about the cabin like trapped barn swallows and I closed my eyes to the sound of Feo running so fast downwind.

The sun had dropped in the pale summer afternoon and the giant maple trees in front of the house tinged the light coming in the barn door a pale green. A swallow trapped above the hayloft darted back and forth with flashes of pale brown, searching for a way out. My brother's hand clutched a length of lathe about the size of a schoolboy's ruler, as he stalked his prey from the floor. The bird swooped and dove and darted downward just in time to clear the underside of the pitched roof.

Suddenly Geoff's shoulders turned and his hand shot upwards in a perfect throwing motion. The lathe mimicked the swoop of the swallow to converge with it in the darkness and the two of them plummeted straight to the floor at our feet

"Wow," he whispered. "Now that was a shot."

The bird lay lifeless on the floor, the death-dealing stick only inches away.

What made you think of that? Brody said.

You asked me a question. I was thinking about attacking myself, wondering if I attack myself. Suddenly I was in the barn and the swallow was trying to get out, and with this miraculous throw that was little more than an act of boredom, the bird was dead.

And you felt guilty? Frightened? What?

No. Awed by the sheer improbability of it. That little stick flying up to snatch that bird out of the air, the swiftness of its death. I was amazed and awed that my brother could defy the speed and aerial acrobatics of the bird — like he knew something Aboriginal, that somehow the wood would mimic the bird's flight.

He knew that a simple stick of lathe could simulate the flight of a swallow in the dark.

You love your brother?

Are you asking me?

You do love him.

He made me learn to throw left-handed, even though I was right handed in everything else, because he couldn't hit left-handed pitchers in Little League, and this would make me a better pitcher. What had he ever not done? Held me down to drool spit on my face until I cried. Taught me to box (partly so he would have a punching bag). Put a choke hold on me until I gagged. Led me deep into the woods so he could abandon me in tears. He came home as captain of the soccer team he started in boarding school, with 10 other players to live at our house for a week. Then there was the time a couple of older Dumont kids caught me alone on the road and beat me up with a log. Geoff was just 16 and happened to be home when I came home in tears with the back of my head bloody. He took me down to old man Dumont's house and demanded that he apologize to me for what his boys had done. The old man was maybe 50 and tough like the lifelong carpenter he was. He made it clear our physical safety was on borrowed time if we stayed another second on their front lawn. Geoff left a threat in the air that he might take revenge at some later time.

I said to Brody:

I can't reduce my feelings for my brother to a simple sentence.

Well, we are just speaking. There are other forms it could take.

I get confused sometimes about who is talking here and who is listening. I was trying to get to tell you something about my brother.

— And I interrupted, Brody said.

Yes. I was looking for the beginning.

Which is what brought us here, he said.

Yes, I said.

I am sorry, he said. In all the hours we had spent together, Brody looked abashed for the first time.

Voices spoke amid the gurgling water tanks underneath and words gargled in the throat of the galley sink.

"Well, okay."

"Really?!"

I went up to tinker with the vane until it held Feo on the 275 course for Kahoolawe, still 40 miles off, so I could sleep for a while.

Τhe ten-mile strip of deserted munitions dump on Kahoolawe that had been used for years as a U.S. Navy bombing target spewed clouds of fine red dust into the wind. I dozed as Feo drew closer. The high black cliffs came up like a shadow in the sunset to begin a perfect, clear night. The heavens were unmarked by clouds anywhere. I forced myself to do exercises in the cockpit and gulp down chocolates and black coffee. The wind grew shifty and began to drop into a quietude Feo had not known for days. I felt her slowing.

Kahoolawe held an eerie quiet feel, silhouetted against a distant amphitheater of lights that had to be the southern face of Maui. I kept squinting at the compass and tinkering with the vane to keep us on course. The land off to starboard was all dark, flat fields, telephone poles and roads running in parallel to mark property. People came out on verandas overlooking the water. Sounds rose of a cocktail party, a wedding reception. Feo's passing had became the subject of intense discussion.

There is no waterfront in this open water, no people. Yet I see them standing in the darkness. They cannot be.

Falling asleep down the companionway steps, my hands rose instinctively to grab the edge of the hatch before my face hit the combing.

By 10 p.m. Feo had rounded Kahoolawe and I stared across 20 miles of water to another inverted bowl of pinpoint lights. A white light flashed every six-and-a-half seconds. Did that mark the tip of Lanai, or was it some impostor?

You missed it. It's some other light.

What other light?

No other light around except this light. This must be the light.

I searched on the chart for another explanation and found none. I kept adjusting the vane and dozing as the wind shifted south, weakening, as Feo crept on.

At last she came close enough under the flashing light for me to perceive the shape of willow trees hanging down to the water. The breeze died off and left a second night sky lying where the ocean had been. A lone house appeared on the waterline. A car came and went. The Pilot warned of long periods of calm between Kahoolawe and Lanai.

Becalmed on this last brink Feo drifted under the roof of stars, bright enough to illuminate my hands in front of my face. I scanned the midnight radio for a local weather report. The Eagles began singing "Desperado" over a Molokai station.

"Desperado, why don't you come to your senses?
You've been out riding fences, so long now.
It may be raining, but there's a rainbow above you.
You better let somebody love you...let somebody love you...
You'd better let somebody love you, before it's too late."

The song unbalanced me to the brink of tears, and without the strength to stand or even sit down, I lay back among the sails to stare upwards.

"You can't reheat a soufflé." My father's voice.

The voice in Desperado ran to the beach house. Another car departed up the waterfront road toward the place where Kaumalapau must be. I fell asleep until the light came on.

A dawn breeze played across Lanai's sweltering stone bluffs to the east, then whispered up from the empty ocean to the south. From this angle the island appeared flat brown and barren like the prow of a wide ship approaching, a flasher on the metal tower at one end. Apparent buildings beneath the light were revealed as hallucination. Continuous steep tan cliffs along the water caved in to a sudden dent not far west, marked by white steel fuel drums. Through the binoculars I could make out tiny men at work at the harbor's edge, a crane moving on a barge. My nail-bitten fingers were stinging, salt-sore, on the wheel. The sun began its climb up my back, tropical heat rising toward noon without relief.

My top lip is blistered from yesterday's blasting sun, I notice it in a few singsong words uttered to encourage the wind.

"Why don't you come to your senses? You've been out ridin' fences for so long now..."

Feo moved parallel to shore until she seemed unable to draw closer. I can't stand it anymore. The damaged engine will give Feo some headway, I calculate, and create apparent wind with our momentum. The diesel labors and chokes itself off almost immediately. I do not dare to restart it. Burning hot and becalmed, I am still unwilling to go overboard to swim.

Don't ever leave the boat, Dad said. You never — ever — leave the boat.

I draw a bucket of fresh water to douse my head.

I will put the dinghy overboard, lash it to the stern, fire up the tiny outboard and inch Feo into the harbor.

The dinghy is over the side in the water, I am leading it aft on a line as a voice in my head cries

"Don't drop the line, don't drop the line!"

An unseen force strips the line from my fingers and drops it into the water.

I have lost the dinghy overboard in flat calm! I rush aft

"don't fall overboard, don't fall overboard!"

to bend over the lifelines and climb down onto the self-steering frame to stretch my hand after the floating line just as it inches beyond reach.

The dinghy drifts away quickly and seems to accelerate where there is no wind.

———————

It grows smaller. Now only a dot.

I am out of control.

A few hundred yards astern some men in a fishing boat have their poles out and lines in the water. I had not noticed them before. I manage a shrill whistle through my fingers and they look up to see my arms flapping skyward. In a few minutes they have brought the dinghy alongside. I hand over the unopened bottle of Johnny Walker Scotch I had been given for emergencies.

"Best thing we catch today!" said the one wearing a Greek fisherman's cap. Their boat wheeled off amid a chorus of laughter.

I did not trust myself to step into the dinghy and mount the outboard. I hung grimly to the wheel and played Feo into every faint hint of air that rose. After several hours she crawled within a few hundred yards of the Kaumalapau beach.

My head felt baked, my fingers swollen almost immobile. I thought of the offshore zephyrs that sprang up in Cape Rosier whenever the little sailboat approached our mooring off the porch. My mother called this "our anchor breeze."

"I could use an anchor breeze, wherever you are," I said aloud.

A small figure set indelibly into the background, she looked now across the water from the porch toward Buck Island, as she had watched all those years before. She had been there my whole life, except for times when she might have been defending me but was not.

"I know you're thinking of me," I said.

Up from the south the water darkened with a puff that now moved Feo gently into the only open space within a small fleet of fishing boats at anchor. I went forward quickly and pushed the anchor through the bowsprit. The chain uncoiled in an accelerating roar over the side.

Feo lay with several small dories moored at her flanks. Kaumalapau rose on three sides, stratified clay bowl of red and white. The shadow of the land brought silence all around, marked only by light air whispering over the cliff-top and the wash of waves on the beach. A cave mouth gaped in the cliff wall. Two tugs nestled against an ocean barge at the quay as a crane hoisted containers aboard. From that loading area a narrow road curved uphill. Lanai City, the yellow cross-hatching on the chart, would be that way.

Too late for Emily to fly here. After sundown in Penobscot Bay, my father would be waiting for the call. What could I tell him?

Barely able to move my arms, I began to furl the mainsail and mizzen, the canvas painful to touch. Voices of men and working machinery drifted across the water.

I did not want to let go of Feo yet but slumped on her foredeck, letting her come to rest within the southerly curve of this little bight, where she now lay under the thatched and feathered brown and green hilly landscape, in a spacious silence marked by an occasional distant vehicle crackling across gravel. Here and there were visible clumps of Pili grass that had once made the island invaluable for roof-thatching material. I remained still for the longest time, taking measure of Feo and of the land around us.

II.

Closer to My Heart

"...Where we had thought to find an abomination we shall find a god;

Where we had thought to slay another we shall slay ourselves;

Where we had thought to travel outward, we shall come to the center of our own existence;

Where we had thought to be alone we shall be with all the world."

Joseph Campbell
The Hero with a Thousand Faces

Almost two decades later, I found myself sitting in Feo's aft cabin, trying to reattach a miniature Chinese chest of drawers that I had bought in a Hong Kong antique store to decorate the renovated aft stateroom. I removed the small but different sized drawers one by one — all eight of them — so that I could attach the chest to the bulkhead furthest aft. There it would face the cabin and contain a variety of small parts and special objects I wished to keep close at hand.

Here in the smallest drawer was the charm that sailed to Hawaii with me, a fisherman's lucky coin now wrapped in tape, which I wore around my neck all those weeks, some 50 days in all; extra masthead light bulbs; a miniature seascape by the artist father of a former girlfriend; and then suddenly, to my surprise, in another drawer all on its own, was the small, oblong box of arbutus wood that held the last of my father's ashes. I had bought it at a craft fair in his boyhood town of Ganges, British Columbia, when I had traveled back there on my mother's behalf to scatter the final third of his ashes in the harbor where he had spent his youth. The top of the box had split along the edges and come free. I opened it gingerly to see whether any of the ashes had escaped, and also to see whether the box could be mended. I was surprised to discover on top of the ashes a tightly folded piece of white paper, with a note in my own handwriting:

Yea, though I walk
through the Valley
of the Shadow,
I shall fear no Evil.
I love you, Dad.

The sight and perhaps too the sound of these words, which I heard myself reciting aloud in a quiet, broken voice, brought me to the verge of violent tears and I stood up quickly as if to suppress them. I knew this physical sensation all too well and could never be sure where it would lead. I learned about it in the years while he was alive, as well as in the wake of his death, though the nature of the feeling had changed of late. There had always been more beneath the sensation than I felt able to contain or was prepared to release, even if I could say exactly what it was. That I should find myself here alone in this moment in a Maine boatyard, preparing to put Feo up for the winter, and have this come upon me after all that had intervened since I put his last few ashes in the box with the note — whose very existence I had forgotten — was itself a mystery, and perhaps the very mystery on whose trail I had been all along.

Who or what exactly had he been to me, after all? I had not known what to feel about him in the end. And in the wake of his passing, now more than a decade old, I was still trying to figure it out, struggling to finish the story of my sail to Hawaii and what it had meant. Was something about him always to reside in me in this congealed but struggling-to-dissolve form? Would it find a way to steal upon me whenever I happened to confront his memory, invoked by coincidence or circumstance? I now felt as much blessed as cursed by these tears, which — or rather the feeling beneath them — was forcing itself up into my throat like solidified vomit on the rise. Trying to support myself by grabbing the post in the center of the cabin, I felt the powerful urge to overcome the sensation as it came upon me now. It had persisted on its own terms through the years and had refused to be resolved. Now somehow it demanded that I go back to the story I had struggled with since his death. What I had once thought was only about the sailing, or sailing and the two of us, had become as much about the journey afterwards, or things that stood in the way of telling it, or that blocked my understanding of what it was — or perhaps all of that. Did I hate him, finally, as he accused me after he read the story that first time? Or were my feelings for him still struggling to find authentic expression in the wake of his death, and my mother's deterioration and the accident that half destroyed my brother? I was now in the declining stages of my third marriage, my son was about to turn six, and this sensation, arising within me as I looked upon the final ashes of the man who had brought me here, seemed to be a signal. Perhaps I had come to the place from which the ending could be written at last.

The girlfriend whose artist-father had painted the little oil seascape that I could never bear to give up had always said that to finish the sailing story after my father's death I would need to go somewhere alone and write — and cry — and write. That was the only way that I could ever hope to find the end of it, she said, to let go of it, whether I was ever really done with it or not. She said I didn't need her, as I thought I did, but rather some belief in myself that had always been missing. I could not be sure just what she meant. She had loved me despite my drinking but declined to align her life with mine for that and perhaps other reasons that she never acknowledged. Now at this moment she came vividly into the cabin and I felt grateful to her for having urged me to embrace the tears and follow them wherever they might lead. For as much as they had threatened to engulf me — I felt that if I ever let them out fully they would rupture my body into pieces — they might also set me free.

I had not fully appreciated when I arrived in Kaumala-pau in the calm dead heat of that July morning and reached Norman the foreman's shack above the harbor to call my father — for his was the voice I most longed to hear and the one response I sought more than any — how deeply the sailing thread wound through both our lives and bound me inextricably to him. He had been convalescing on the porch in Maine for much of my trip, worried about the outcome, that much I was sure.

"Well, you made it," he said matter-of-factly. "It took you long enough. You sure had your mother worried." I heard him cover the receiver to shout to my mother somewhere distant in the house before he came back on the line. "You'd do better to have someone with you on the way home."

"Yes, well," I said, feeling the tiredness of the last few days at sea break over me in a wave. "I got here. It might get easier the second time."

I could see him on the porch in perfect detail and hear the subtle reproof, which I might have predicted in some form. Whatever he may have been feeling in my favor he did not express. I learned later that he spoke proudly to his friends about my passage, even as he intimated that I was a fool to have gone alone and would be even more misguided to return solo. If I wanted him simply to cheer for me now it was not to be, and I could not say why that was.

Something about him in this regard had come to me, strangely enough, when Mauna Kea and Mauna Loa first appeared through the clouds in the final days as Feo and I were closing in, searching for physical signs that we were about to arrive. Everything known as "The Big Island" was visible above the water, but all that lay underneath — thousands of fathoms of ridge and valley, an unknown mountain range all its own, which if you drained the ocean away would make these the earth's tallest peaks — was forever, irremediably, obscure. You might dive on these mountains and underwater valleys, but however far down you went would never be far enough down to grasp them. You would unearth more questions than you would ever find answers for. And this would always be true of my father, a towering figure in my life about whom so much would remain impenetrable to me. That came clear now in the perspective that distance from land and maybe my first 25 days alone at sea somehow afforded. Looking at those mountains I was stunned by them as symbols of all that I could never know.

As much as I wished to leave him behind and get free in some ways yet to be known, he had come along as tangibly as if he had been aboard — along with all my ambivalence. I needed to experience the ocean alone but I wanted to share it with him, too, and he was the one I wanted to reach first upon landing. What was there about bringing him along and leaving him behind that drove me equally? I had needed to put a whole continent and 2,500 miles of ocean between us to see my own intention more clearly. I had to pursue this solo adventure even as he counseled me against it. And I was far from finished. Doing it solo was meant to be some kind of antidote, as I had suggested to Joe Miller. The path of fear was solitude itself, but I had found myself to be far less alone than ocean solitude implied.

So many thoughts and feelings had come aboard with me, along with intense memories and confusion that dogged me. I had gone back over old ground with Brody in new ways, on the strength of our session tapes that I brought and listened to intermittently on the way to the islands. What did I hope to find in them? I had visits from various important figures in my life, including a few women I had loved but been unable to stay with, for reasons I could not explain. It was mystifying how my mother showed up at the end, when I was desperate for an anchor breeze and called upon her to bring me in the final few hundred yards. Norman said he had been amazed and astonished to see me sailing into the harbor at the last because no breeze *ever* came up from that direction on a summer day, not *ever*, not even *faintly* in his 20 years of memory. I felt more ready than ever to give myself up to things that could not be explained, or that were simply out of my control. And I was about to meet a man who was transforming the island where by chance I had happened to land, who would speak to me in ways like a father and give me a piece of advice that would help me immeasurably to keep going.

Dav. id Murdock's office in the Dole complex was rich with pale yellow orchids when his secretary admitted me at last. A sequence of Asian brush paintings of Admiral Perry's historical landing in Japan circled the walls and a copy of "Land and Power in Hawaii: A Contemporary Political History" lay prominently on the coffee table. Then a very short man in a black pin-striped suit entered quickly through a side door. He had a small face with sharp dark eyes and big ears, and his left ear held a tiny beige hearing aid.

He thrust out a gnarled hand. "David Murdock," he said. He reminded me of a gnome, with a graying and balding head slightly too large for his body but rendered prominent by those dark eyes. His heavily lined face suggested hard thinking and maybe hard drinking as well.

I introduced myself, told him quickly that I had sailed into Lanai alone from San Francisco. My deal with the paper had been to find a good economics story in Hawaii while I was here, and I thought Lanai presented a compelling story about a way of life in jeopardy. Or so it appeared.

I had toured the staked-out site of Murdock's proposed 200-room lodge and 17-house compound, complete with would-be croquet lawns and a pheasant hunting preserve in the highlands. By local and newspaper accounts, he was an intense, modern Horatio Alger-type motivated to possess all that his impoverished childhood lacked. He had barely extricated his mother from a water-heater fire when he was 16, a tragedy whose injuries killed her by degrees. Stories said the boy promised himself to get control of his life and never lose it again. At 64, as a one-fourth owner of Castle & Cook, he had orchestrated the $600-million conglomeration of Dole, Oceanic Properties of Honolulu and Flexivan, his original company, and made himself the second largest landholder in the Hawaiian islands, behind Bishop Ranch.

Some detractors considered Murdock just another corporate raider from California, expert at what commonly goes on in the application of finance capital. His development had become Lanai's latest experience as the victim, or beneficiary, depending on your view of it, of foreign powers. In its known history the island had been ravaged by Hawaiian warriors, bought by Australians and proselytized by Mormons. For the last half century the island had served as a plantation of Dole Pineapple, which used Kamaulapau to off-load the crop to canneries in Honolulu. Now that local pineapple wages were two-and-a-half times those paid in the Philippines, this plantation was about to be retired and become a resort for the very, very rich.

"Some people there feel the place has totally lost control of itself, of its historical essence, and even its reason for being, except to serve a distant master and to be fed upon by strangers," I said.

Murdock stripped off his jacket and sat down on the couch to face me like someone preparing to lecture a small boy.

"Let me tell you something," he began, his head cocked to favor his hearing aid. "I resent being called a takeover artist. When I bought it, Castle and Cook was in monumental hemorrhage — $267 million in debt and no way to service it. In default. The banks had filed for involuntary bankruptcy when I read about it in the Wall Street Journal. Three weeks later I pulled it out of the muck it was mired in. I gave it new life."

He paused to enjoy this analysis and went on.

"I've been a builder all my life. Houses. Businesses. People. I try to teach people to change their mental image that says they can't do something." He pressed forward like someone collecting himself to leap into space.

"Anything a man's mind can conceive, a man can do. It's an old adage. Whatever we think we are in our mind's eye, we are. That we can become. Most people see themselves as less influential than other people. That's their problem."

He leaned toward me in a way that reminded me of the Colombian plastic surgeon I met at the Hotel Lanai who dismissed Lanai as an island of beer squalor, a culture totally destroyed by ours. Dr. Uribe had a way of presenting himself as the man with all the relevant facts, and he was very bitter about losing the only place where he could shoot deer whose flesh tasted of pineapple.

"We become what we want *if* we have the courage to *do* what we would most like to *be*." Murdock said "if" and "do" and "be" like drumbeats in his statement, which came out as a fervent hiss. He cocked his head further to emphasize what I took to be his core philosophy.

"It's simple," he said. "*Act to be.*"

Before I could respond he pressed on.

"It isn't hard to be in business, it's hard to do a good job. It isn't bad to have an ego, it's bad to have *no* ego. Are you following me?"

"Yes," I said. Could he see himself in any sense as a despoiler, however well meaning, of a way of life? Some of the poorer residents had no chance of ever buying a house and just wanted to continue their simple lives of pineapple-growing. They just wanted to hunt and fish and enjoy their beach as they had for scores of generations. Rich *haoles* had no idea what it meant to be possessed.

Murdock frowned and his voice rose. "That island was beautifully primitive when I came and I expect to maintain that. Each hotel will have fifty landscaped acres of Asian graveled walks and orchids of all kinds. We will maintain the 120-foot pines on the mountain as a cathedral of contemplation, a place to think and relax and enjoy the five senses. Did you go there?"

He was referring to a stand of pines planted by Lawrence Gay nearly a century ago. Gay's grandmother, New Zealander Mrs. Elizabeth Sinclair, had bought private rights to the island from Hawaiian King Kamehameha in 1864 for $10,000 in gold and bequeathed it to her family. Lawrence brought sheep and cattle and a variety of trees from Australia in the unsuccessful effort to establish a ranch. He was a passionate plant lover who imported pines, and cultivated sandalwood, gardenia and Koa, the local mahogany.

"Yes, I heard someone almost bulldozed the pines under by mistake," I said.

"Should've fired his ass," Murdock bit off. "My desire has been to change the land as little as possible except for the hotels, and keep the rest primitive. I know of no other place in America where one can wander 90,000 acres owned by a single company. The thought is not to create a hotel environment but a place for self-inspection and relaxation."

"Plus certain amenities?" I said. One fear was that the hotels and ornamental greenery and golf courses would suck up all the island's water.

"Yes, of course. It will include two polo fields and five croquet lawns, and a pair of Jack Nicklaus golf courses." These he seemed to dismiss as the words came out, but he flushed quickly with pleasure.

"I absolutely love it," he said, eyes gleaming. "Of all the things I have done in my life, this is the most exciting. I am involved in every single detail — design, landscaping, right down to the stone used in the walkways. I enjoy the chance to do this on Lanai, not only to get away, but because of the control."

Norman had told me that Murdock, within minutes of getting out of his plane on his first visit there, had looked around the beach at Hulapoʻe and something about the place hit him hard. He wanted to turn it into his definition of a better place. Maybe the world's biggest Pebble Beach.

A sudden thought now possessed Murdock and his face became strangely livid.

"You!" he said excitedly. "You understand this, what it means. You went out and proved something you'll never have to prove again."

"What's that?" I said.

"That you can imagine and dream and then do something. That you are not a coward. And now you own that. You can take it with you anywhere you want to go."

He leaned back to gaze at the images of Admiral Perry's arrival in Japan.

"We are not so different, you and I. Most of the things in my life I've imagined, I've done. I have 400 head of horses. I'm an outdoorsman. I don't look like it, do I?"

"Not exactly," I said. He might have been a jockey in another life, probably a very good one if he had the hands for it.

"But you do come across as somebody who sets out to do whatever he wants, and does." I had already concluded the plantation manager was right. Murdock probably could talk a starving dog off a meat truck.

"You bet your life," he said. "But only because I do it. I know there are people who say we are destroying their way of life. But when it's done and finished they will reluctantly say I

---

have improved the quality of life in Lana'i. That's what I really want."

I had come prepared to dislike him as an icon of finance capital pursuing its own interest without regard for anything but its own return. And maybe he was. But whatever else he might be doing, he was living his passions.

And he was right that I had been changed in some way by the passage across. I could feel something I could not yet explain. Maybe if we had met before my crossing he would have been more intimidating to me. I couldn't say. I was now more curious than ever to know what made him the way he was. Did he have an opinion on how to tell a story about sailing alone for people who might not particularly care about sailing?

Murdock looked through me with a curious affection that seemed paternal.

"Yes," he said. "Give a chronological story of your fears. Ask yourself the most personal questions and try to answer them. People will listen to that."

All my journals from the past five years remained unopened but I had brought them for a reason. Something was in them that I had to find, or that had to find me. Sometimes I thought of it as the center of my own existence, if there could be such a thing.

I was not going to abandon this private passage in midstream. What point was I trying to reach? An explanation for all the rupture or discontinuity I felt in my life, feeling my way along a wall, looking for an opening that never appeared, or falling through spaces that appeared unexpectedly, perhaps of my own making? Was that it? I felt compelled to press through this next period of exposure and isolation that was entirely mine, not something I would owe the paper or anyone else, and try to open it up, or open up to it, whatever it was.

"Listen to yourself," said Don Michael, my oldest and closest friend, in one of the phone calls I made back to the mainland, perhaps hedging my bet that I would return as planned. I wanted to make sure I touched base with the people I cared about most.

"You didn't get there on a fluke," he said. "It's unfolding this way for its own purpose, and that is your own, whether you know it or not. Everything that got you there will help bring you home, and then some."

I took his words as my own best impulse trying to make itself heard. Typing frenetically in Feo for several nights to meet the newspaper deadline, I felt myself drawn toward a new life, whatever that might be. Buying Feo — a move closer to my heart, as I now understood it — had encouraged me to follow my fear of solitude, which started me down a path that was still incomplete. Murdock was right. I had acquired a new strength that might take me anywhere I wanted. But at the time I could not say just what it was.

Still, I fought a sense of foreboding and repeated my own mantra of that time. Get clear. Decide what you truly want, for yourself. What really matters? I did not know how to be more definite, or honest, or more non-committal.

Then I had a long talk with Em, who had just received the day-by-day cartoon calendar of my journey across, which I had mailed from Lana'i.

"I like when the engine stopped and the little Stick Man said 'Darn!'" she said, with a musical little laugh. "He's funny. And the Moon and the Spoon in June, I liked them too. When will I see you?"

I encouraged her to count the days and try not worry for at least eight weeks. A grizzled old Vancouver sailor in a nearby slip did not believe I could match Michel's time of 19 days from Honolulu to San Francisco, logged into his chart five years ago. His pencil-smudged fixes showed him turning east on his eighth day and noting a violent storm on the fourteenth. Then he and Feo went on to San Francisco apparently without incident. I could expect to stay on a starboard tack for nearly 1,000 miles with nothing to do but tend my precious and inexhaustible steering vane, read and write and sleep and dream. I knew too that I had to fight my tendency to slide into dark moods by disciplining myself with a firm schedule. At first light, breakfast of instant cereal and raisins. Peanut butter and jelly for lunch just before the noon shot, tea at 4:30, no matter what. Chicken or vegetable curry, the sundown meal. I was tempted to conduct my own private race against Michel, who in some ways had put me here, but I did not want to rush to end something that had taken me so long to discover.

I kept resisting my father's insistence that I find someone to accompany me back. I was not finished with the solitude, and I now knew one thing for certain. I was not afraid to be alone. I was good at it — maybe too good at it for my own good. The challenge was to be with others over time, and try to get close, and stay that way without destroying whatever it was we had together. Whatever had to be resolved in me had come aboard with me — the sense of blackness I could slip into if I were not careful, a dangerous slow background noise with the capacity to swallow me up, and high speed anger that could become rage beyond my control. I had felt these in pure concentrated form with no one there to trigger anything. I could not blame or put them off onto anyone else. If it was not the fear of being alone, then what?

S ometime in the middle of the fifth night out — 12:25:50 GMT, as I wrote it down moments later — Feo stopped in the water. Motionlessness and an odd silence woke me with a start.

Reins dropped, the walking horse stops to graze.

I came up into that strange quietude with a taste of metal in my mouth. The vane blade wobbled strangely against the pale starlit sky. The jib and staysail flapped oddly in a mild breeze. The hull felt caught on something underwater.

Feo was stuck in irons facing dead into the wind and wallowing. Something had quit working.

I went aft and shined the flashlight down behind the rudder. Something like a long narrow fish flashed across the gleam of light behind the stern — the broken blade of the self-steering, bent up at 90 degrees. A few minutes of wave action would soon break it clean away.

What did Pete say? Self-steering always breaks. No help for another 2,000 miles, the hardest yet to come. How could I cover the distance alone without it?

I re-attached the tiller cables directly to the cockpit wheel with loops of bungee cord steadying the wheel. A line of bright stars, the ecliptic path of the sun, carved an arc to the east. It was 3 a.m.

My father tinkered with Candida's main sheet, slacking and tightening, and played with the jib sheet at the same time, drawing it in and letting it out bit by bit. We weren't far off Cape Porpoise, Massachusetts, and he wanted to teach me how a sailboat could sail herself to a given wind angle — the old way. After a while, the tiller relaxed amidships and Candida went straight on, her bow held off the wind by the pressure of the jib as the mainsail worked to turn her back upwind.

"There," he said, "You see? Balanced. There's a spot of natural balance. You find it and take advantage of it. Sails working against each other will keep her on course as long as the wind holds steady."

Feo whispered along, stern pressed down by the mizzen, bow held off by the jib. The reefed main drove her in balance between the two. Feo hardly needed any help to keep to the course. *If the wind holds steady.* It would not last for 1800 miles, that was for sure.

One thing broken set fears in motion about other things that might break. *What if* the rudder bolts sheered, and Feo lay helpless? (I had heard that strange clunking again through the floor of the aft cabin.) *What if* a floating ship's container punctured the hull? *What if* the mast cracked under strain?

Maybe I should turn back the 500 miles to get the vane fixed. Pete said he had been quickly exhausted after his steering system quit, and he had two mates to help him. But Joshua Slocum had sailed around the world alone with no wind-vane. So had others. I still had Pete's book and the surgical tubing.

And Candida was a sloop. I would make this work better in Feo, with four sails to balance.

No. I did not come out here to turn back.

Under my makeshift system Feo sailed meanderingly west of north. Noon sights and dead reckoning came easier. Once we closed within about 500 miles of California — in theory at least — the Loran would quietly take over. My new Hewlett Packard calculator, bought second hand in Hawaii, asked for the angle of the sun, the date and time, and substituted lightning calculations for my own error-prone math. It could produce the sun's ground position accurately within seconds. Fear of mistakes and confusion dissolved. I ran the repaired engine for an hour each evening to recharge the batteries and was comforted to find no leaks. The repairman in Oahu said it might last until San Francisco this time, even though this Yanmar cooling system was a known liability.

❀

Solitude, by Anthony Storr, had come into my possession by chance in Honolulu when a former girlfriend of my editor at the Examiner, who worked for the Star Bulletin, appeared on the Alawai Yacht harbor dock with a going-away gift just before I pulled away.

"Our mutual friend suggested I give you something to think about on the way home," she said. "I hope it's not too lonely."

In one's dissatisfaction with the "habitual self," Storr was saying, we encounter areas of self-understanding that elude our grasp. He emphasized the difficulties of finding solitude in a world beset by telephones, radio, TV and sensory overload of all kinds. Our patterns and habit tend to get us where we are. (I knew this from growing up in a dairy town where a local showed me how to tell time by the cows, which will always be in the same part of the field at the same time of day. He suggested that many people, particularly small town people, were like that too.)

One way to explore the self was to remove oneself from present surroundings and "see what emerges." No one could tell whether this disruption would lead to better patterns or to deeper understanding, Storr conceded.

Feo went along smoothly in 15 knots of northeasterly in the early evening, driving her rail down to sudden puffs, as I sat reading. The smell of onions, frying with potatoes and corn beef, rose out of the cabin with the strains of Mendelssohn's violin concerto in E minor, my mother's favorite whenever she was troubled by something. I turned the concerto up full on the cassette player.

How many hours, days, weeks of her later life had she stood over the sink in the kitchen as my father sat reading two rooms away? He had "seen life and sat down," he told me. But she was still standing there. Sometimes I thought that washing dishes had become her most comforting companion, that or the half-full glass of wine and a cigarette, and, more and more often, Mendelssohn playing from the distant room, counterpoint to the silence of that old house.

The cooking smells wafted up from Feo's galley. Wind tumbled across the corners of the hatch with a muffled tearing sound, the pan clanked as the stove caught in the gimbals and evening sunlight shot through the port side portholes.

...and her listening reached past the portrait of her that they won as a first prize in a Manhattan waltz contest during the late '30s. In puffed sleeves off the shoulder of her blue evening dress, she was darkly coiffed with the short hair of those times and blue-eyed and she evinced the hint of a serious smile. The pose made her look uncomfortable even as she appeared so graceful, an expression that oversaw all our family dinners, and their fights, and the portrait now resided as a marker of the distance between them. He sat in his TV room with the morning Globe and Times crossword puzzles, and her listening followed the music through the back hallway, past the narrow rear stairway to the library Victrola that he bought as family Christmas present years ago. Above the fireplace hung the seascape she had painted of the skiff rescue off Cutty Hunk one summer — no one aboard — and claimed as salvage, fruit of Candida's chance passing.

Feo's bow crunched through the chop. The Tibetan chimes rollicked in their clinking and horizontal shafts of hot light rose and fell with the clamor of the French horns. The piano melody descended lightly like water coursing into rivulets. James Joyce had said of words that sound was their first meaning and to know the root you must listen to the heart. For some reason this made me think of her, so small and at the center of the house, surrounded by the silence that throughout my childhood, and ever since, I could not cure or fix, except by finding the music she wanted to hear, and leaving her to it.

Later, if people asked me "what was it like?" I would not be able to say it in words: everything, and all at once itself.

Sailing northwest in Feo's belly into this empty, open space, as geographically far from land on an ocean as the planet allows, my own journals seemed to lead me back onto a route started some time before. I felt myself finding bits and pieces like crumbs dropped along a trail I had not wanted to lose. Following them as the ocean carried me further into this empty space, I marveled at how certain elements had converged, or had hung on to bring me here.

I had gone to Harvard on a journalism fellowship to study capitalism, and I did not like some of what I discovered. Capital would find ways to concentrate itself, and then concentrate on returns, at the expense of all else, including individuals in the system. Top executives would tend to extract far more than they deserved, aided by boards compensated for looking the other way. Middle managers would fight tooth and nail for dwindling opportunities in the hierarchy. The environment would be used up in imbalances, in the defoliation of rain forests, global warming from industrial and auto exhaust or the desperate wood-cutting among the starving in Africa. A level of disparity, either social or environmental, would eventually arise, perhaps enough to topple the system itself.

The world was compelled to serve what a prominent American lawyer, who had practiced corporate law in Tokyo for 35 years, had described to me as his only true client — "the forces of concentrated industrial capital, disembodied from national interest." Corporations were in thrall to the power of global capital in pursuit of financial return. Subject to these forces, individuals and communities would find themselves increasingly disassociated from deeper human needs. The system would invite exploitation and undermine common purpose. How was the individual to defend against that?

Suddenly my father was hospitalized to check for nerve damage and determine his heart function, which had begun to fail the day he retired. Seeing him in sudden decline was to feel the ground coming out from under me. I was not alone among my contemporaries in the Baby Boom, many of whom were losing their fathers to illness or death at about the same time.

Able to look out over the pollution-deadened Merrimack River, not far downstream from his old office and the nearby Lowell Sun, where I had taken my first newspaper job, he aged perceptibly day by day, alone in a bare, cold room at St. John's Hospital. His doctor said he was unaware that my father had been consuming two to four and sometimes more cocktails per night for decades. Now he would have to quit drinking to give his ailing heart a chance. So he did — just like that. So I did too, and began to feel a change in myself. I began to drive out from Cambridge in the evenings to rub his back and get his circulation going.

"It's not hard to quit drinking, you know," he said ironically. "All you need is a doctor to tell you to quit." It was his way of telling me to consider it, because even though he did not think he had a problem he was quick to suggest that maybe I did.

I wanted to get inside that circle you made with alcohol. You often seemed alone and afraid, at least before you got angry. After a decade of my own drinking I thought I understood your habit. Slow the mind down enough to get off the thought train, the clack-clack-clatter of thinking that seldom slows and never stops, or dull the darkening plain of feeling that steals upon you in silence, even when a room is full, and you can only see a single flower on a tie or a nail on the floor or a shoelace and all else falls away in the distance. I thought I knew that about you, but maybe it was only something I knew of myself.

Just then my mother came into his hospital room. She had been telephoning me in Cambridge every morning to report his condition, and her own. The house seemed so empty. The dog knew something was wrong and wouldn't go into his kennel. She was falling asleep when she least expected it. Sometimes when she stopped to think of a word, no word came — only a color. With two daily trips to the hospital, how could she find time to paint? When she came into his room now and saw me with him, she gave me a stricken, distant look that turned toward the window and the river.

"Oh," she said absently, "I should have been doing that."

On the arched metal bridge where Route 113 crosses the Merrimack River at the Tyngsboro town grocery, I pulled over to write down the words, "To My Father in His Final Illness," the title of something that would capture what his sudden decline had let loose in me. Maybe it could acknowledge what we had been to each other in the best times — so much of it unspoken — and to tell my own version of his rages and early brutality, which everyone seemed to pretend had never happened. It was to be an honest tribute before he died, a journalist's own version and maybe proof that I could write my way out of a trap set years before.

Classmates had been volunteering how their fathers had made marks on them too, from which some were not yet free. One was 19 when his father collapsed of a sudden stroke, an old baseball player who burned his arm up too soon and never made the majors, then spent his life looking back. His son feared to lose his own future in a morbid fascination with the past as might-have-been. Another recalled vividly the day he discovered his father, in advanced stages of alcoholism, passed out in a pool of blood and vomit just before his son arrived home from boarding school. As a 14-year-old he delivered his father by cab to a Maryland hospital and left home for good, never to look back except in fear of his own drinking, which stretched from afternoon beers through dinner-time hard liquor to late-night brandy, in which I often kept him company. A third watched his workaholic father sink into bouts of manic depression, and already sensed it in himself. All their stories made me wonder about my own. What was I doing in these studies, in journalism, drinking and dreaming about some other life while my first marriage was collapsing?

"Maybe the image you have of yourself as a human being is tremendously limited," said Bill White, the Harvard Business School capital markets professor who was trying to help me understand the nature of finance capital and wealth in the United States.

"Maybe your image is tied to labels and stereotypes and fears of the ego, fears that in seeking higher levels you will be rejected or fail," he said. "If that is so, then the process of the self depends on the pursuit of the spirit, rather than being pushed along by other human beings."

Professor White had, in his study of uncertainty, produced elegant math models about how capital markets should behave. Now cancer was proving how quickly one's own blood could turn fatal, and as the final uncertainty swiftly approached, he looked for answers in a spiritual question. What part of him would die, and what would live? His Catholicism meant more to him now than all his impressive scholastic texts in finance. He urged me to think more deeply about the legitimate pursuit of self-interest, and to find a way to write about it.

Emily's mother had decided to return to her own work in California, taking Emily with her, and leave me to finish the spring semester on my own. As I felt things coming apart I was desperate for something to hold onto. In the psychologist's office above the Charles River, I had kept running into the same wall of fear and grief but could not find the heart of the matter. I could observe myself in periods of my most persistent drinking, vaguely hostile to all things, and suspicious, wondering why so many conflicts arose.

"Families that mask honest feeling with liquor and anger blind their children to feelings as they truly fit together," said the Charles River therapist. "You need to stop and work on that."

Then it is in here somewhere. The voice doesn't depend on any audience but on oneself. Only I stand in my own way.

For whom was I writing these journals, whose ear? I tried to imagine a time coming, wrenched free of guilt or parents or fear of failure, when it would begin to fit together.

Something would unfold.

Within a few days of the end of his life, Bill White looked up in his empty hospital room through a maze of tubes and recognized my face. Fear in his eyes, lips tinged with pink froth, his chest rising and falling with shortened breaths, he managed a smile as my hand closed around his.

"One last note... from the professor," he whispered through the hint of a smile. "You may fear to write those things you think will be used against you. There is the risk of ridicule

---

or being unloved, obstructions to writing what is truly in your heart."

"Fear is in there somewhere," I said, and marveled at how he could speak of mine at this moment. His eyes seemed to be seeking mine as he spoke again.

"You do not need to believe in my God to seek your own spirit," he said.

Hours after he died, I took a long walk up Park Street near Boston Common, past a horseback patrolman and guitarist against a wall, uphill past two postmen on a lunch break, a bag lady, two lovers on a bench, struck by all the people around me in his sudden absence, a man I had come to revere as "a found father" and example of something spiritual in his style of teaching. I fought a moment of panic that my fellowship year had been wasted, that I had not accomplished nearly enough with my time. Yet I had been given another key to unlock routes into myself, generous words spoken from his deathbed, to uncover fear and loneliness that had to be faced in order to ask, *what do I want out of this moment, which generates fruitfulness and self-worth, if there is to be any?*

Returning through the Cambridge Common, I stopped to write something about how family should reside at the human center of things, bring love and truth and a host of human virtues to bear, the means by which we might hold ourselves together against the world. The words expressed more hope and desire than anything I felt able to do for myself or anyone else at the time.

I wrote then: *you are stuck trying to keep your boat from sinking. It is all you have, you and yours, with the heavens above and the deep below.*

Balanced along a northerly course with the elasticized bungee cords holding the wheel, Feo went on for one slow, quiet day after another. Time itself was slowing. Embraced by the unfolding of this ocean and the fish that rose and fell, I grew calmer, and moved with the stealth of any man walking naked in a place where he might slip and fall. I was completely withdrawn into the heart of my journey as I could not have imagined it from any distance. The lesson of the first leg was that things are as they are, not as we wish them to be. I was not in control but subject to chance developments that could render all previous plans useless. I would not try to fit the future into some idea but absorb myself in the present and remain open to each successive moment as it came. A certain deep relaxation overtook me then, some great weight lifted off.

Sitting on the aft hatch I sang with an instructional tape of Rudolpho's first-act aria to Mimi in *La Boheme*. I strained for high notes in tortured Italian until a school of porpoises surfaced to object to my strange vibrations. I was now feeling altogether open to the sea and through successive nights and days felt myself dissolved into that limitless horizon, conscious of growing closer to home, whatever I might make of that at last.

There is no one with me and yet everyone, in whatever form I bring them along.

Above a range of underwater mountains known as the Prokofiev Seamounts, we were just past Handel and on our way to Donizetti, an underwater peak at 1,549 fathoms, due east of Bizet. Beyond were Schubert, Rossini, Verdi, Wagner, Stravinsky, Mahler, in that order, with Shostakovich further out there on his own. Struck by these depths I had a sudden, desperate attack of wanting to see Emily, and went below suddenly to write

something to her that came upon me fully formed, and which I
wrote quickly, start to finish:

The Deep

What could possibly be
at the bottom
of the bottom
of the deep blue sea

so far from you
so far from me?

Could it possibly be some monster
that nobody's ever seen?
If there were such a thing,
would he be kind
or would he be mean?

Maybe he wouldn't be he at all,
but she.
Could that be?

I wonder these things
as I look to the deep

that bottomless place
(like my mind
when I sleep)

I imagine
sometimes
it's quite beautiful there,
home to elegant princesses fair,
grove to sea blossoms utterly rare.

If there is something living
way way way
way way
way
down there,

does anybody care?

I do.
And if you ever find out, please tell me.
I'll keep it secret.
(I swear.)

At the time I saw this as a simple poem to amuse my child. But in the years to come I would come to understand it as much more. It contained a question that had been raised by my early family experience, obscured from me as it was from others. Perhaps it had inspired me to be a journalist, as it would later occupy my life as a business consultant. What *was* the secret in the deep — my own or anyone else's? If you found out, would you tell? Would anybody care?

In dead calm I took off the sails, the moon a sliver in a sky matching the ocean. The horizon vanished, sky and sea grew indistinguishable except for the stars as they appeared. Feo melted into this setting, a single vessel joined with the phosphorus, reflecting all that came upon her. The thought of all the time I had missed with Emily brought me to spontaneous tears.

The clouds had drawn an indistinct continent, dappled Percheron grey to the east, with cloudless blue above. The wind came up softly, and with it a languorous swell barely perceptible, a football field rising a few feet and then moving along for the next, coming to take its place. From radio WWV in Hawaii a faint woman's voice announced coordinates that meant we must be just rounding the Pacific high pressure system. What were these little creatures floating by, transparent half dollars erected like little sails? They looked like pacifiers for infants in the sea.

Storr was saying that in Henry James' "*The Beast in the Jungle,*" the beast lying in wait and so greatly feared was the simple act of falling in love. Jung was speaking of his own mid-life period after he turned 38, divorced, and broke with Freud.

"The years when I was pursuing my inner images were the most important in my life," he said. "In them, everything essential was decided."

He conjectured that men who became neurotic at mid-life had been false to themselves in some way. By scrupulous attention to the inner voice of the self, the lost soul could rediscover its proper path, as he believed he himself was doing. The attitude required was almost religious, although one did not have to believe in a formal God.

I had tried to be settled in a marriage before I was settled in myself, seeking companionship in place of something else that was missing.

Jung found many middle-aged patients "not suffering from any clinically definable neurosis, but from the senselessness and aimlessness of their lives." He wanted them to embark on a process of individuation, whose goal was a sense of wholeness, to find "an attitude that is beyond the reach of emotional entanglements and violent shocks — a consciousness detached from the world."

He encouraged them to find time for reverie and to pay attention to paths suggested by fantasies and dreams.

In this faint wind Feo kept turning herself about and trying to sneak south during the night. To quiet the noise of sheets and blocks banging I took the sails off and tried to connect the old automatic pilot. But the wheel shaft had worn itself out of round and I couldn't get it to work. So I abandoned the idea of using the engine and went back to reading, determined to outwait the doldrums.

The ocean is asking me to take more time.

The apparent aimlessness of calm persisted. The galley sink gargled incontinently, a rude background to sleep. A mountain of grey clouds rose to the south. The radio reported a typhoon 500 miles east of Japan. I read a snatch of lyrics I had written for no apparent reason:

> *Would I ever tire of the sight of you?*
> *Would I ever begin to make light of you?*
> *Would I ever get over my fright of you?*
> *Honey, I don't know.*

On the aft hatch at midday, I was startled to find myself joined by a British Royal Air Force colonel in full dress uniform. He resembled my Uncle Gordon, second of five sons and the one who might have been a twin of my father, photographed in his RAF uniform during the war. That photo of him, ramrod straight, had always occupied a place on my mother's bedroom dresser.

"Who are you, and for that matter, what are you doing here?" I said. I was no longer particularly troubled by hallucinations on board, since I had been told on good authority that this was the first symptom of serious sleep deprivation.

"I'm your alter ego and I will be with you for a while. Coffee at six, porridge at nine, sandwiches at noon, tea at 4:30 and dinner at seven. Ham, jam and spam will do very nicely. Remember that discipline is your best defense against depression. Stay on the clock!"

"I don't mind your being here if you can be useful," I said.

"I can be bloody well useful," he said. "I know more about your family linen than you have ever been told."

"Really?"

"Yes, indeed. Your Grandad was a sweet liar of a great story-teller who made tall tales, good beer and bad business. If he hadn't taken up with a young chippie in Ottawa he would not have spent the last 30 years of a 65-year marriage sleeping in a cabin separate from the main house on that God-forsaken island. Your Grandmum, like any good daughter of a High Church Episcopal priest turned missionary nurse, kept the family together through the sheer force of personality, sparing the rod not at all, I can tell you. These were qualities that served her bloody well in the private war over whether the youngest son was her husband's, or someone else's."

"You're joking," I said. "Those five brothers look like subdivisions of the same sperm cell."

"Righto, but your Grandad suffered private agonies. Shellshocked from the first Great War, he came home to look upon his latest offspring in a light that was not true. Chased your

Granny around the place with a loaded .22 until your 13-year-old Dad took it away from him. But that did not stop the dear old man from suggesting, in not so subtle ways, the youngest son did not belong."

"Is that why the eldest son of the youngest son became a sharpshooter?" I asked. On the occasion of the 50th anniversary in Ganges I had once watched as that cousin — he must have been six or seven — was slapped consecutively by his father until he responded dutifully "Yes, sir," to his father's every question. I wondered if this had helped him achieve his Olympic stature on the Canadian national rifle range.

"Yes," said the Colonel. "Nothing motivates fine riflery like suppressed patricide. Punitive qualities in the father, visited upon the son, are visited upon his son, and so on. We are the living legacies of all that came before."

He vanished then, just as he had appeared. When I tried to write down the entire conversation, bits and pieces escaped me as if I had just awakened from a dream.

T he book that Pete handed me just before I left San Francisco with his prediction that my wind-vane would break was full of diagrams and explanations of what happens to a ketch in various wind conditions and how to use sails to steer with the tiller tied into a makeshift system of lines and elastic cord. This I had already done.

The author described several systems of pulleys to bring the staysail sheet along the windward side to the tiller. The tension of the sail on the tiller would be counterbalanced by surgical tubing. This equilibrium could steer a very accurate course on most points of sailing in steady air. Downwind was another matter.

I rigged several blocks as directed. When the staysail filled, it pulled on the sheet, which pulled the tiller, and tried to turn Feo downwind. The trick was to find the exact angle of sail, length of sheet, and tension in the tubing that would hold the helm steadily on course. It was engrossing to tinker with various points of adjustment to make the system steer consistently. Doubling the surgical tubing inside a small pulley made it hold the tiller firmly. This took almost two days to work out.

Feo behaved like an old horse asked to perform under a strange bridle. Too much tension on the sheet bore her away from the wind by five or ten degrees. Too much tension on the tubing made her luff up into the wind, where she stalled. And so it went for hours at a time, too loose or too tight, back and forth, until her wake in that mild breeze left a meandering frothy track like "a snake with a broken back," as my father used to say. I was first learning to steer Candida downwind in rough weather, discovering that if I gently let her have her head, she would often come naturally back on course.

The author cautioned that much patience and ingenuity would be needed but that time would be well spent for any single-hander who could not be glued to the helm. "Do not lose heart if the system does not work the first time, because a solution can always be found," said the text, and I was grateful for the counsel. I sailed on with these tasks and ideas in my own monastic seclusion, expanded by the vastness as it came over me.

A luminescent blue shark with a gaping horizontal mouth slid under Feo's bow at a 45-degree angle, waved its tail in silent grace and vanished as quickly into the green. A boat-length ahead, an upward flick of silver broke the surface and arced back to the water. A tuna, tail up and head down. "Plot!"

The water went still.

Persistent flashes of these jumping tuna, glistening amid occasional bits of floating trash, had been rising and falling for a couple of days. Feo had become a fish-aggregating buoy, towing my fruitless lure astern. I believed these jumpers were only curious about the passing hull, or happy to have company.

A flicker rose up and a thrashing disturbed the surface as the fish disappeared as quickly. Perfect silence returned with the calm.

A few feet ahead of Feo's slow motion now the blue stealth reappeared, parallel gill slits fibrillating with the flow of water as the lean body accelerated out and upwards into the dark water again, unblinking eyes set prominently on a body of cold intention.

Not far off, a pair of fish leaped as silver flashes above the surface. The sound of the tuna striking the water came back as a faint "platt-ash!" A pregnant moment of silence fell. Up went another, toppling back. Thrashing ruffled the water.

From the foredeck their sequence acquired a hypnotic quality. The sky went blue to lavender.

The shark was barely visible, criss-crossing methodically under Feo's bow. The fish kept going up ahead, falling back. Before long I could hear their rise and listen for the imminent thrashing. Their perturbations so close around, the shark using

Feo as his accomplice, having the advantage, knowing the end, drew me inside the circle of their struggle.

Draw a line from this spot on the earth to the sun. Looking back from that distance, ask yourself: What is the difference between living things?

They are nearly indistinguishable.

This moment of recognition arrived as if from outer space.

The shark is hunting and the tuna struggling to live and the man is watching. What distinguishes us is motive, our intention. What makes me different are those things I pursue. I am what brings me here. What brings me here is what I am.

The definition of my life lay in this. In the end I would be whatever impelled me. Four lines appeared in my journal at this moment:

Clarify the intention
Define the sacred
Understand the commitment.
Act to be.

Just as Murdock had said. This last one hit me like a heavenly bolt from the blue.

D onald Crowhurst was the English inventor who entered the first single-handed around-the-world race in 1968, immensely inexperienced and ill prepared, compared to fellow competitors like Bernard Moitessier, Robin Knox Johnson or Nigel Tetley. They had all spent their lives learning what a boat could and couldn't do, and how they needed to prepare for the relentless and potentially overpowering conditions of the open ocean. Crowhurst had hurried to leave on the *Teignmouth Electron*, his ill-conceived trimaran, soon to discover in the mid-Atlantic the sheer impossibility of what he had set out to do. With one hull leaking and numerous other failures aboard, he made an illegal stop in South America, then came back offshore to pretend — through prodigious mathematical computations — that he was rounding the bottom of the world with the others and sailing with the fleet for home. Compelled to race by his own business ambitions, but forced to continue because of financial contracts that would bankrupt him if he failed, Crowhurst could not face the audience and promises he was unable to keep. As the fleet began to close in on him and the magnitude of his entrapment came clear, he stepped overboard, apparently believing himself able to become divine, at last at one with God.

From Crowhurst's journals, discovered aboard Teignmouth Electron after a ship came upon it weeks later, drifting emptily at sea, a pair of London journalists pieced together his unraveling in their book, *The Strange Last Voyage of Donald Crowhurst*. I had bought it in Alawai just before leaving, without knowing the story or the influence it might have on me alone in the ocean. It underscored the British tradition of individual heroism, or the fame achieved through extreme voyages, of which Ernest Shackleton's foolhardy attempt on the North Pole was among the best known. Insistence on the stiff upper lip, suffering is an antidote to sin, death before dishonor. Pain builds character. Better to die, to be lost, even to give up one's family, as Crowhurst did, than to reveal an embarrassing truth.

From time to time I would be seized with fantasies about him, or they would seize me.

Towering, billowing, bulbous grey-stocking clouds hung mountainous ahead, the first hint of a weather change. Pale mares' tails streaked the blue sky like splayed fingers of a giant hand. A faint ring partly encircled the sun. *Halos predict a storm at no great distance. The open side of the halo tells the quarter from which it may be expected,* said the weather book. So I should watch out for trouble from the east.

After almost two weeks on the starboard tack, held north by the uncertainty of not knowing whether I was now above the high or might be overtaken by it again, I was growing anxious to turn east. According to his penciled markings, Michel had encountered his gale not far from here. I should stay north to catch any wind shifts to drive me a bit higher, since the common misjudgment was to turn east too soon.

Feo crept on towards the grey mountainous sky to the north, dark curtains of rain falling beneath. The Pilot chart indicated we should be nearing the top of the high at 37 degrees North, nearly even with San Francisco. Feeling blocked, suspended, helpless, with no whitecaps for more than a week, I sensed an imminent change.

A rain mountain would drift west out of our path and bring another evening like those repetitively passed, last gasp of faint wind at nightfall, clouds darkening to embers in the distance, a peened leaden ocean without a hint of variation. The brown bird had returned — the same distinctive, prehistoric arch to its wing, evolution refined to a perfect equilibrium to the motion of the sea, the wind, and the object of its predation. How preposterous a man must seem with this huge, stiff imitation of a wing, yet we were joined in wind and air and gravity that gave us both rise and motion.

One morning the wind fell and tried to rise again, the swells strangely crossed. Long, large rollers from the west cut smaller lines rising from the southwest. The two vacillated like stagecoach spokes on film, moving in a backwards illusion across the surface. Scores of porpoises followed like dark curved needles sewing the surface off to port as thick white thunderheads bundled themselves up to the east.

My journals were spread out below and I felt the eerie presence of Crowhurst, a man who had lost himself in himself somewhere and a victim of the audience he both knew and imagined to exist. The lies about his position that he telegraphed back to England caused others to press so hard for the finish that Tetley's multi-hull broke up and sank, though Tetley himself was rescued. Moitessier, second to Knox Johnson at that point, suddenly abandoned the competition and headed halfway again around the world for Tahiti, declaring that life — not competition and not fame — was the real purpose of life. His book "The Long Way" would become a cult classic for ocean sailors everywhere.

The barometer began to fall as the wind rose mildly out of the south-southwest. Within the next 24 hours whitecaps were everywhere and the barometer fell another four points to 1017 in as many hours. I stayed on deck almost continuously through the night to adjust the self-steering as the wind kept shifting south, and rising. Feo was soon running off the wind at seven knots as we knifed through that seamless dark. We were now on a course of about 65 degrees, just east of northeast. With the set and drift we could expect in the final 1,000 miles, as the prevailing north-westerlies and heavy seas set us southeast, we were aimed for home. The barometer had now dropped 6 points in 12 hours, but I had no real sense of its portent, too preoccupied by the sail and line and tubing of my self-steering working in what seemed perfect collaboration. However inefficient, this was more satisfying than the wind vane, and I took it as a sign of my progress.

Feo was traversing the freighter lanes shown on the ocean chart to extend from Panama to the Philippines when a sudden sensation took me physically by the throat and dragged me on deck, where I could breathe more easily. A premonition of being run down, that was it.

Something is going to get in the way.

I couldn't spot anything in the binoculars. The Coast Pilot described gales, heavy fog, swift currents and crowded traffic zones to be expected closing in on the Golden Gate, but we were still far out. Unsettled, I forced myself below to make coffee. A flying fish had flown aboard and died in the scupper just outside the galley porthole. Its greenish brown cigar shape released a mysterious stench. I caught the whiff of propane near the stove, a burner turned on by accident, inviting explosion. A mysterious creak arose from the foot of the mast. A clunk *(what is that?)* clunk *(what could that be?)* clunk *(something in the rudder is working its way loose!)* would not stop resonating from beneath the aft cabin.

The account of Crowhurst going mad gave credence to mental deterioration aboard. How would one know if it began to happen? *These attacks are normal.* Everyone is afraid, deep down, of the inevitable day they don't make it home.

What if we knew we were not coming back?

A snowy petrel appeared, gliding back and forth above the deck on currents of this new wind.

"Say hello to Em for me!" I cried out. The bird gave me a look before wheeling off. Did my sudden grip of fear signal something in the distance? Emily's grandmother had been ill with lung cancer. I pictured Emily's mother at her funeral, crying over all I knew was unspoken between them.

My father's raspy voice emanated from the porch in Maine.

"If you wonder if it's time to reef, it's time to reef!"

There must be something in the air. I went below and switched on Channel 16. I gave Feo's vessel number, coordinates and destination.

"Anyone in vicinity. Do you copy?"

Silence.

I fingered my fisherman's charm, fire and sky, circle within a circle within an octagon, the shapes of unknown magic, and made tea, the English antidote to all discomfort.

"Don't worry," sang McFerrin, "Be happy..."

The barometer was off another point. The air had turned chilly and thinner on the skin. I was too tired, had forgotten to eat. Discipline waning, now my imagination was free to play low blood-sugar tricks on me. I knew better than to let myself slip, with no one around to help.

The log meter ticked frenetically through the night as Feo hit 10 and 12 knots in gusts that rolled her up near her beam ends. By morning the seas were eight to 10 feet high and curling up over her starboard quarter, some breaking as they came on. Feo had made 171 miles in 24 hours! Our personal best, and I wondered what speed Michel would have been making under the same conditions.

The southwestern sky had turned to dirty engine oil, sworled on a dingy yellow canvas. I changed Feo's course to cross the seas at an angle and tried to tie another reef into the main. But the mainsail slides jammed as usual and I didn't dare turn her sharply for fear of being taken down sideways by one of the big seas that were now breaking around us. I got the Yankee jib down into the bowsprit and wondered how long I would last at the helm if the staysail had to come off, since that would disable the mechanical self-steering.

Wind shifting south meant a low-pressure system was moving east, its center somewhere close. Feo was running with thunderous rushes now and I had to steer her around the breaking combers as they arose through the afternoon. Moitessier's book warned against letting the full-keeled Joshua come down the front of a steep wave too fast because she could bury her nose at the bottom of the trough and pitch-pole, end-over-end. By early evening the barometer hit 1010, the lowest I had seen it in 45 days, but the seas steadied at this height and I fell asleep right after dinner, despite myself.

Quiet woke me.

Feo had gathered herself up as if she'd inhaled deeply and was now holding her breath.

No wind.

No shrill rigging or any hammering through the hull alongside the quarter berth.

Dead quiet.

I threw the hatch open and came up quickly to catch in the corner of my eye the pale boom swinging violently across the cockpit just above me, the sound of the wind sweeping back with a shriek, then black air engorged with rain driven sideways. I ducked as a sea struck Feo's bow and slammed her so violently that she pitched me onto the cockpit floor. The boom shot overhead and the hatch crashed shut, just missing my right hand.

Up on one knee I peered into the dark to windward. The gale blew my eyelids open and drove them full of salt water just as a giant hand grabbed Feo by her rigging and twisted her violently down on the port side. The deck went up at right angles and I slid down under the wheel, reaching up to head her up into the wind. Everything was black, shrouds mewling and an overwhelming gargle close at hand as if we were being swallowed into the throat of a giant. Water incensed the air with lashes of rain and another squall hammered Feo down as I tore away the self-steering lines to regain control of the wheel.

Out on the bowsprit the wind ripped the jib clear of its lashings and blew it overboard as the staysail flogged with the crackling sound of small arms fire. Mainsail and mast went pale in the downpour and I was on my knees, clutching the wheel to my chest, trying to turn Feo up to reduce the pressure off the main, begging her aloud c'mon, please, c'mon!.... *She will not break and if she breaks she will not sink.*

Feo rolled, lifted up to starboard, then pitched down sliding and falling, the dark rising endless roll up from the right, eyelids lifted if I looked up, and sudden water in my mouth, drenched shrieking sound of the lines and staysail banging and cracking and lines lashing, *turn turn get up hang on Feo,* unable to reach up to windward, the *crack crack pow pow* of explosions from the foredeck, eyes adjusting to follow the line of the boom into the seething dark, dark jib now unfurled and dangling, tipping and sagging overboard like a sea anchor waiting to be filled and carried off *no no don't go up there with no harness hold on get her nose up let it go let the fucking jib go!*

The wind and rain and Feo's steep sailing angle are pinning me down, afraid of being swept off if I rise above the line of cockpit, she is twisted up to windward by the pressure and I do not dare touch the main sheet under this tension, *must slack, no choice, where is the topping lift* now unhinged from the end of the boom and flailing an invisible steel fitting on a wire near my head somewhere. *Keep her nose up, don't let her fall off and turn down, slip it slip it c'mon baby c'mon get up get up don't break you can do it okay okay don't look to windward, head down, hold the wheel tight, hold the wheel... No. Lash it down,* Pete said.

Trembling broke out in my shoulders. I don't know how long I had knelt there, been held there, rainwater pelting and coursing down my chest and back, my T-shirt and sweatpants soaked in ice-water plaster, sea thunderous with collapsing hillsides, great walls of dark water rising up from windward and sweeping beneath her in the dark.

Feo rose and fell on these enormous inhalations of movement, the intermittent break and roar of a sea turning white above her and pounding down on the deck or sweeping down around me in the cockpit as green water swirled into the self-bailing holes around my knees. She was not going to go over if I could keep her at this angle upwind, the mainsail now slipping the gale. My teeth began to chatter and I couldn't stop my shoulders trembling.

Gotta get below get something on.

I waited for something to change. A silence would fill in with the instantaneous hesitation of the wind, then flail back down on her and *I am helpless without help or companion* and names and faces swept through me of everyone I ever loved and would not forget, my father at the helm, flashes of Emily and her mother and...

Another fiendish gust struck and rolled her down as I yelled at Feo to encourage her:

"Hang on, Feo, hang on here –!"

sure death sinking down into cold noise and darkness.

The mainsail thundered explosions up and down its height, then filled in awful quiet as Feo fell over before each gust. Her bow tunneled into dark green water that enveloped the bowsprit, swallowing the bunched jib and breaking back, crests of green water exploding along the deck and hatch as she met the seas full on.

I waited for the mast to crack. Salt blind and trembling from the cold and fear of helplessness at the end, I felt penetrated by the perfect knowledge of how easily the ocean could take me whenever she wanted.

Sea doesn't care, I am nothing to her, do not exist she can take me when she wants me doesn't care too small not here yes I'm here not here to die not to die to live hang on Emily Emily Dad loves you I did not come here to leave you Emily hear me now.

Another burst flattened her and Pete's voice kept telling me to leave her turned up, lash the wheel to hold her.

Get below, you're soon dead if you're too cold, it's hard to come back from that cold once it really gets into you.

She was hove to now as much as she could be, and I would see if Pete was right: *you can always heave to.*

In the dark below I stripped and scoured myself with a towel until warmth come back into my skin, found dry clothes and then bundled into my wet weather gear and harness and went back outside.

The night had dissolved into water and sound. I couldn't face the moaning wind with open eyes or perceive anything beyond the dark shape of the jib sagging to leeward and the staysail flogged to pieces, ripped open along each seam. Feo was moving on her own wisdom and instinct. She took a steep angle up the incoming seas before they could overcome her bow, holding herself steady, and enabled me to crawl forward, belly down on the deck awash to furl the jib into a tight bundle beside the anchor. I had no hope of bringing the jammed mainsail down further and thought it foolhardy to try.

I harnessed myself into the cockpit. Feo rose up and tipped down over these seas, her masthead light a tiny beacon unto itself, hardly making any headway but holding her position against the charging waters. *We belong to this ocean as it possesses us.* An occasional wave broke up her bow or windward gunwale to send another dark, explosive curl rushing along the deck.

How invisible we had become! I retied the lashing on the wheel and felt the crushing desire for sleep. Nothing I could do but give up to it.

I crawled through the galley passageway to the aft cabin and burrowed deep into the leeward berth under the only dry blankets left aboard. My fear was strangely dissolved into an acceptance I had never known. The darkness behind my eyes, the dark of the ocean, the sense of Feo's innate capabilities and my own swirling thoughts took me deep down, resigned now to this furiously indifferent night.

I woke to the pungent smell of wool blankets and the salt scent of wet animal hair. The ocean was uneasily smooth with a fish oil gleam beneath dark low clouds. Under single-reefed main Feo was ghosting west in a weak northerly. The staysail hung in tatters.

Having aimed for the edge, I had come to it at last. I had tried to abandon the sense of who I had been and this one night — to which I had given myself up or was utterly taken — had stripped me naked. On my knees and chilled at the prospect of the end, I had seen myself laid bare before whatever God there was, and there stood people I loved. The power of the ocean had washed away regret and bitterness and I felt cleansed, as if everything I meant to leave behind was now truly behind, and all else lay ahead. I had been given what I had not known to ask for, just when I feared myself lost.

Content to go nowhere as the wind fell off, I stowed the wrecked sail, ran the engine and made a batch of shortbread. By mid-morning the grey pulled back to leave brilliant blue dotted puff white, and the barometer jumped back up to1020. I tuned in to Radio Moscow and Australia and caught snatches of the Republican National Convention in Dallas. The engine batteries would only recharge so far because the alternator belt was slipping and I had no spare. The smaller and stiffer storm jib in place of the wrecked staysail would not work as responsively in light air, but I was happy to sit in the sun and relish the day.

The dots of white folded into themselves overhead and Feo languished in slow motion as I gazed across the calm.

There!

The tip of a mast above the horizon, directly aft, overtaking. How odd, that the only sailboat to come upon us in weeks should come up just now. In another hour I could make out a cross-spar halfway up the mast and knew who it must be. This boat had left Alawai two days ahead of us and we joked about racing boat for boat to the mainland.

"Aha! Feo! Do you be*lieve*?!" A voice cried out exultantly from Sausalito's *Evening Star* as the double-ender drew within a few boat-lengths. A tired looking trio studied me intently from the cockpit.

"What're the odds?" I yelled back. This apparition had me doing a small dance on the aft hatch.

"Unbelievable!" came the captain's voice from under his white cap, his face all smiles. Over the radio he confirmed our position, 37:16 North Latitude and 146:23 West Longitude. They had sustained some rigging damage last night, both crew violently sick. Better now. Falling behind their delivery schedule, had to press on. Good luck to me, too.

The *Evening Star* receded slowly eastward and I felt overcome by solitude, wishing they had either stood by for a while longer or not passed at all. The short rendezvous reminded me suddenly that the Japanese character for "human" is the symbol of a lone figure among others.

Have I been to the heart of the heart of you?
Have I seen the very best part of you?
Do I know both the craft and the art of you?
...Honey, I don't know.

Southeasterly rollers built for the next several days as the wind climbed to 25 knots and steadied. The barometer fell a point and a ring encircled the midday sun. I listened every hour to WWV Colorado for any hint of nearby gales and began reviewing the nature of Pacific storms.

Extra-tropical cyclones travel in families of two or three, taking 24 hours to reach maturity and several days to dissipate. A thickening or lowering of the cloud layer means wet weather coming. If the wind sets in between south and southeast, and the barometer falls, look for a storm from the west-northwest, passing to the north within 24 hours. The speed and degree of drop in the barometer will signal the speed and power of the storm. In the storm just passed, the wind had clocked from southeast to south as the barometer fell 15 points to 1010 in three days. The worst wind struck after the barometer bottomed, after the center of the low passed directly overhead. Then the wind reversed direction and doubled in force. So it caught Feo from the opposite angle at about 65 knots just as I came innocently out of the hatch to explore the silence.

I had been in the eye and not known it.

Expecting trouble from this southerly, I tried to calculate from Moitessier's description of Pacific typhoons whether I should change course. The weather report put gales 1,000 miles north and moving northeast. Moitessier echoed my father's advice when Maine conditions turned ugly:

Start the sheets and run!

So I turned Feo as far downwind as I dared on a northeast heading. Oily seas grew steadily taller for two days. Feo shot along at a steady eight knots with the double-reefed main, storm jib and yankee, like a farm wagon careening downhill. From time to time, one of the bigger following seas caught her stern and forced it across the wind toward the jibing point, but each time I reached the wheel to steady her. After a while, this motion worked its way into my awareness until that particular yawing motion alone would wake me from a sound sleep.

The self-steering cannot be trusted alone.

As Feo drove on we listened to rousing applause and laughter over the radio as Republican Senator Robert Dole at the National Convention mocked the "Du-cock-eyed ideas of the Governor from Massachusetts." Gov. Michael Dukakis had been silly enough to suggest that corporations should not be completely free to pull capital out of dependent communities.

Maybe he was onto something, even if he couldn't sell it into the machinery. The "wealth-creation" popular in Reaganomics depended heavily on borrowing from the future. The seated government occupied a stool on three legs — financial capital, individual gain and adversarial law, so the absence of cooperation would develop as a natural condition. Americans were taught to extract or consume whatever they could in a society built on sophisticated alienation — individuals given over to the larger machine, with concentrated capital operated on the principle that the relatively unregulated pursuit of returns would best serve the whole. The law separated church and state while commingling business and the public interest. This was the heart of Reagan's deregulation.

Where could one find an effectively challenging voice in the mainstream "free press?" Once proud of its First Amendment guarantee and its status as the Fourth Estate, the industry now championed individual wealth and profit, and advocated humane conditions for the displaced as an afterthought. Family newspapers were being swallowed one by one and quickly digested by globalizing corporate interests. Fewer and fewer voices of real dissent would be found within the media conglomerates, now among the most profitable U.S. companies, and champions of corporatism in their own style.

How can one be in it without being of it?

Every worker, village, company and principality was vulnerable to takeover in some form or other. Little wonder that people had an uneasy sense of losing control over their lives. Yearning for a less striving existence, where inner experience would be more important than material achievement, people sensed how easily they could be bought or sold. How many knew enough, or could afford to ask where this was all going, much less imagine they might change its direction? The degradation of the environment was just one sign of larger machinations, working against basic human interest. The modern citizen opted out, but took refuge in TV and media, consumerism, a drug of choice or work without meaning. What did it mean to pursue health in a sickening environment?

Many people were trapped on their own islands. Home rule was a ready victim of corporate economic force. *Ready to be possessed, like Lana'i.* Monetary and property transactions governed. There were cold realities at work behind America — acquisitiveness, corporate management from afar, deepening inequity — in effect a bleak national identity. The dogged pursuit of economic self-interest had taken over something larger in the collective soul.

Until an outraged Laniian forced him to build a few houses in that remote community, Murdock was the exemplary American entrepreneur, well armed with lawyers and accountants, unfettered in his use of capital. Yet any corporate possession like his was itself another island, ripe for sale or expropriation.

Whatever his campaign failings, Dukakis was trying to raise the issue that corporations couldn't act unilaterally in the local marketplace without some mechanism for taking others into account. And the Massachusetts governor was having trouble. As long as enough people were getting by, it would be nearly impossible to confront the corporatization of life, or the true influences of global capital let loose on the world. Nor would the powers-that-be give any credence to Dukakis' most un-American question:

How free should capital be?

Pushing the Reaganomics he once decried as "voodoo," and vowing never to raise taxes, George Bush would be elected under the business-as-usual banner. But a global sea-change was afoot. America was in danger of faltering in its own global commitment to finance capital and multinational corporate self-interest let loose. To retain legitimacy, a democratic country would have to make more than it spent and maintain fair social value for the majority. History might well look back on the Reagan-Bush years and conclude that they sowed irretrievable seeds for the next Great Crash, or Great War, whichever came first.

I awoke to Feo's thunderous progress on a broad reach heading east, mesmerized by the rise of the full moon behind scudding black clouds. Above this huge and tattered sky the planets shone in a staggered row to the east, primitive pointer to the horizon where the city lay a few days further on. Cloud-enshrouded and lividly full, the moon itself had a faint halo that put a mercurial patina on the sea. Through racing apertures of those clouds in flight the moon shot down like a spotlight lancing into a darkened stadium. Odd shapes raced across the water, lively winged creatures of silver in search of something to light on. All at once the moon broke through to inflame Feo's mainsail like a giant petal, translucent in sunlight after the rain. This sudden illumination bound Feo to the sky and I saw myself moonlit, awestruck, seething with her onrush, the hull a metallic porpoise working mightily with each driven wave to dive, dive deep into the deep. The light fell across the rolling dark oil froth of the seas, Feo's steaming wake spread out behind like snow dunes and I wrote to my sister that I regretted to be alone just then, amid such wondrous beauty.

The feeling would persist as the southerlies dissipated. The daily breeze picked up from the west, and we came back into the long Pacific swell that hinted some deep continental shelving beneath. The wind shifted to the northwest on a Sunday afternoon and with nothing but easting to make I had a sense of nearing home but with my imagined realization still undefined. My ambition to come back clearer about my life from here on had taken on the quality of a writing deadline, something to be reached before we touched shore. For now I felt content to leave myself open as we came across this remaining space.

After a breakfast of pancake and dried fruit pudding smothered in maple syrup, I had fallen asleep on deck and wakened in time for the noon shot. The sun hit its peak within a minute of its estimated time and the fix missed my dead reckoning by only 14 miles, 360 miles from the last. The Loran, which I had turned on within 600 miles of the city and watched like a television, waiting for it to tell me where I was, confirmed the sight. I was finding my way.

Mysterious and impersonal as its calculations might be, the Loran proclaimed location, direction, speed, elapsed time to any bearing and how much to correct for side-slipping due to wind and current. Moitessier had warned that these devices could be invasive and preoccupying, and cut one off from the universe. The Loran was supposed to help in fog or the dark, or after periods in which celestial sights might be impossible. An alarm would go off within a given distance of a marker. I punched in the coordinates for the Farallons and programmed the alarm to sound within five miles. I saw how it disengaged me from the sky and ocean, even from Feo herself. Later, I would learn what Joshua Slocum meant when he said that the only thing more dangerous than a skipper who isn't sure where he is a skipper who thinks he knows *exactly* where he is.

I finished off a bowl of chicken curry and sat in the cockpit with the sun climbing up my face. I had been dreaming about the storm and had listed in the log the lessons it taught. Believe the barometer. Listen to your gut. Act now, don't wait. Waiting only makes tough decisions tougher, and more dangerous.

If you wonder if it's time to reef, it's time to reef.

Feo's deck gleamed white against the endless blue line of the horizon. The surgical tubing and jib sheet held the tiller on course with quiet efficiency and the sky promised another good night of sailing. Just in this moment I realized:

I was happy to a depth I had never felt before. Not thinking, not struggling to make sense, not trying to force something to work despite itself—just connected to my own heart, back with the boy who under his father's tutelage on the coast of Maine had fallen in love with sailing. I did not know how much this feeling had to do with solitude itself, but I felt strangely serene. *Found.*

Willie Morris, a southerner-turned-New Yorker trying to grasp his roots in his autobiography, *North Toward Home*, was searching for the Mississippi southern boy he had once been. The book had been pressed upon me by an Examiner colleague just before I left San Francisco, "something to read on your way back," he said.

Morris had reflected on writers he had loved, many of whom I had admired as a boy and later as a graduate student of writing. He was now speaking of being southern and born into a system of racism with which he had been raised and struggled to come to terms in his younger life, and later.

"*...Shame was too simple and debilitating an emotion, too easy and predictable—like bitterness. It was more difficult to understand one's origins, to discover what was distinctive and meaningful in them, to compare them with the origins of others, to give shape to them for the sake of some broader understanding of place and experience.*"

His words described a natural human impulse, a point of understanding to which all might hope to come. A sense of one's origins, but to what purpose? What was sacred, wanted, missing?

A more fruitful life that made a difference to people and places I most love.

My parents could not be expected to live too much longer, struggling to reach Maine each summer in my father's failing health. What could I expect to teach Emily about promises and the sacred nature of a person's word? Did giving up the example in my first marriage mean I had to give up the effort? I had yet to show her what kind of family we might create together over time.

Morris had begun to discover the essence of himself as a white from Mississippi, and brought his grandmother and mother to New York City for the first time, an urban landscape alien to two old southerners.

"...the feeling came upon me, not apocalyptically but slow as could be, slow as good sour mash gets its mellowing or as a young man matures and finds balance, that in the great chaos of modern existence it was one's work that mattered, work in the broadest and most meaningful sense — this and being close to the people one loved....the feeling had been a long time coming, you did not have to go to your sources again to survive; one's past was inside of a man anyway, it would remain there forever."

I saw my father, in my eighth summer, standing in the little sailboat after I had begged him to come with me into the darkening afternoon because I needed his weight on the windward side if thunder squalls should blow through, as they were almost sure to do on a day like this. He hiked out on the rail in his red-checked woolen shirt and khakis and grinned back at me as I fought to keep her planing down the waves during the strongest gusts. And in this moment of Feo's steady breath-like movement to the east, the Pacific so apt to its name and blue as a robe in a Catholic mass, I saw his face, younger as it had been then, fade into the Maine background and I felt that familiar choking clot of tears trying to rise.

I knew then that the book I had never been able to start was something about whatever tied us together, in our sailing and our private feelings, which had to be held onto and also let go of, if I could just identify and disentangle the parts. I tried to capture the idea as it hit me then, put something down in my journal about this moment of recognition, as you do when a dream is interrupted and you struggle to capture the essence as it eludes your waking memory.

By then it was nearly nightfall. The long swells looked like the Blue Ridge Mountain hills of Virginia, criss-crossing their own landscape. A moon of Las Vegas neon orange waxed aluminum as it ascended in our path dead ahead. Its light on the water was our path, and under the brilliant line of eastward-making stars I went along in a dream state.

I pictured my father on the family porch in Cape Rosier, gently rocking in the woven-rope and green frame chair overlooking the rocks, maybe watching the Bucks Harbor Yacht Club racing fleet work its way east up Eggemoggin Reach as *Enfin* idled at her mooring a few yards off the beach. How much of his mountain was still underwater, and ever would be? He would be interested in the Pacific wind-shifts coming now, a few hundred miles out, as atmospheric updrafts over the California central valley pulled air masses into the coast. We had come more than three-quarters of the way, above Michel's route and off his pace by several days, and I felt Feo bringing me back to life, though not as I had left it or wished to live it now. What to do with myself when I reached shore was still unsettled and the ocean was not quite finished with me yet. I was still searching for the meaning of the changes in me, and what I might tell him of this passage when it was over. I was pretty sure now that I would leave the paper for good and hole up somewhere and probably spend my last nickel trying to get this book written, whatever it was to be.

Along the 38th parallel the wind shifted into the northeast, pushing Feo south, so I tacked north and the wind immediately shifted back, pressing us off to the west with a spate of potent squalls and oddly twisted seas. After a half-day of flogging northwest I decided to turn back again, but for some reason the seas would not comply. Grey-green rollers from the northwest crossed underneath a northern chop to throw up sudden vicious teepees of water. Feo would begin to pivot when one of these odd waves would snatch her bow and hold it off. Stalled, she lay in irons, pitching face-on to the whistling wind, her hull thrashed like an empty can. Finally she would fall off, and slowly regain speed.

Again and again I tried to bring her about, but each time she refused, or was denied. On the sixth or seventh attempt I heard a torrent of fury:

"Turn, God damn you motherfucker! Turn! Fuck this fucking ocean!!!"

The words broke into a strangled whisper and I realized I had been shouting like a lunatic. I felt utterly stupid, standing there with self-induced laryngitis. Now I wouldn't be able to hear myself talk.

The wind blew in my ears. *It is not them out there, not the ocean and not the boat. It is the nature of your approach.*

Whosoever voice this was, it knew something. Once you looked closely, these long ocean-driven waves were not all obstacle. Each had a peculiar opening in it, with a kind of gate-post on the far end, a conical formation as the ocean swell built underneath. A smooth patch of water trailed these posts, just upwind.

I saw that if I waited, Feo could be steered through the opening and down the backside of the cone as it formed. So I watched for one of these to converge with us, then turned Feo's bow into the gap. She pivoted around the clump of rising water so smoothly the seas might not have been there at all.

I shall always be able to recall in specific sensation the fluid motion with which Feo turned back toward the continent that last time. A sense of harmony descended where I had felt rage only minutes before. Nothing had stood between us and that maneuver except my own fruitless anger and frustration, too quickly gathered and too easily vented, a willingness to blame something for what was lodged in me. How simple it might be if I only got out of my own way and let things be. The nature of my approach, indeed.

"*I can see a school of porpoises playing around the boat and you probably can't hear the noise they make when they broach. I will be quiet and see if you can pick it up*

...shhhhssshshshsshioooe

...brown and white, the size of a man's torso...one, two, three shooting under, you see the flash of their stomachs and then they rise on the other side in unison, a few feet from the bow. One rifles back and forth and underneath, up he comes and out and back down underneath.

A pair is crossing beneath the cutting edge of the bow now, breaking out on the other side. Pooshee! You might be able to catch the sound of Feo coursing along... It's 23:31 in Greenwich, late afternoon in Maine. There go four of them, lickety-split under the bow! I am up on the aft hatch, high enough to watch them playing on both sides, the fifth school that has come to visit on this leg home, the third with opera playing on deck...

There went one!

...Shhshhshhshhhhioooie!

They seem to like Act I of La Boheme, blasting from the little boom-box on deck as they swim past at 10-15 knots, playing tag with Feo in pairs and threes. I keep waiting to see the great white whale."

I held onto a mental image of my father as I spoke into the tape, wondering what condition he might be in when I returned. He might have lost control of the Lasix that kept fluid out of his lungs and be back in the hospital to get it pumped out of his system again. If this were to be our last sail together, I did not want to miss anything. How could I take him to the depths

I had felt across this water? A sense of longing overtook me to bring him here somehow.

Feo sailed beneath black and knotted clouds that wrestled from northeast to southwest, the sun falling down astern. An ominous low roof of dark stretched on toward the continent, precursor to the night. Suddenly the clouds ahead tore open into a small ellipse and a brilliant pond of light appeared on the dark ocean below, like a bright blue hole cut into black ice.

Feo came towards it quickly, or it advanced on us as she advanced on it. In such flat emptiness, a sandwich of pale light between two dark planes, it was impossible to judge how far away it lay. At an uncertain distance off the port bow a mysterious smudge of light materialized. With no point of focus in all this dark expanse except this inscrutable dot, I disengaged the self-steering and aimed toward the color. Feo seemed to want to go there on her own.

The light had the texture of a crayoned campfire in a child's drawing, triangle of orange and yellow and red with a touch of purple down low — like a blaze flaring up in the distance on the desert. It contained a magnetic quality, a diaphanous collection of fiery particles with a positive charge.

Just when it seemed I could reach out to touch that burning bush, a rainbow flowered up from it in an instantaneous arc, across that patch of clear blue and down again to meet the surface no more than a quarter mile away, like the handle on a giant flower basket — a perfect arch above the flatness all around, complete as I had never seen a rainbow before, neither so close nor so continuous, beginning to end. It sped over us as we passed through it, an amalgam of sea and air and sky and light and the distant sun, held together by my eye and mind's eye and penetrating my heart. In a moment we were in the center of that clear pond, spot-lit and embraced from above by the curve of color against all the darkness.

"Oh my God," I heard myself utter. This was the rainbow's end if ever I had reached one. To have come so far to encounter this, whatever it meant, choked my breath off and tears filled my throat like a violent nosebleed. I wept and my body shook. I could not distinguish myself from Feo, or Feo from the water, the water from sky, the rainbow from the excited particles of sight itself, and now the deepest feeling possible. I had come, as my friend predicted, to the realization that I was no less than all that enveloped me.

I tried to recount some of this later for my father's tape, but speech failed to capture it even in the awestruck tone of my voice that night. Maybe he had always found it difficult to hear about these things, or we had never managed to reach into them together and that was what kept me from conveying to him what I had seen, then or later. Maybe, I thought, as time passed and he was no longer with us, that it had been for me to find alone, to discover in a way I could never convey to him anyway. I had come beneath those dark clouds into the aperture that enveloped Feo and me, and under that ring of sky, words evaporated, language vanished — just as they had when Emily was born and I held her in my hands for the first minutes of her life. Alone with that flame and rainbow and changing ocean, the sky opened like a clear lens to the heavens.

"*The space is eloquent.*"

The wind in the microphone whistled, a long surging wash of the bow wave rising behind my voice.

"*It's difficult to convey this solitude, or to capture the ocean. Ocean. The word alone makes an enormous sound, but it doesn't frighten me as it once did. It finds ways to communicate respect. Its total indifference to you is enough to change you forever.*"

I stayed in the cockpit as Feo went steadily east, and collected on the tape and in the log a sense of where I'd been in recent weeks. The winds were taking us where we wanted to go now and we could not miss. I felt much steadier, calmed in ways hard to describe. I reread the logs of this passage, and letters from someone who wanted our love affair to endure over time when I now knew it was not to be, and snatches of the old notebooks, clearer about something I had guarded in my imagination for so long. In the worst of the night storm, certain illusions evaporated. Whatever enduring romantic love was, it had eluded me, or I was not ready for it. Now, after going so far south and working my way back, detached once and for all from the fantasy of the princess, I needed time to absorb the effects — produce something on my own, even if I wasn't sure what it would be, or whether I could finally bring it forth.

The log contained a list of moments that had brought me to tears on this trip: my view from the crosstrees when I had to go aloft to untangle the halyard knot, which seemed so long ago now; the vision of my father grinning years ago in Candida's stern, when he must have seen me against the backdrop of the ocean in a way I had never been before, and I saw into a rare moment of his own perfect joy; my feelings about Emily's divided life, mixing grief over the past with resolve for the future, to bring her with me; the words of *Desperado* off the point at Lanai when I couldn't stand up any more, and exhaustion seemed to crack open a wellspring of grief and release it once and for all; Morris' words, *"a man did not have to go to his sources, it was in him anyway"*; and the rainbow epiphany, if I could call it that, not so many hours before. I had fulfilled something that had been waiting for me to recognize it.

Tears were recognition itself, was that it? Not a source of shame or sign of weakness but a bodily function as expressive as any. The release of feeling, something inside; recognition of desire or sadness or beauty, wordless evocation drawn from some distant reservoir; the apprehension of truth, or utter mystery. Wordsworth's "spontaneous overflow of powerful feeling," as he defined poetry, experienced bodily.

I was learning to face myself and to find a crucial point of listening, to open myself more and to express my own voice clearly for the first time. Morris had reached into that deepest reservoir of sentiment and helped dislodge something already at my heart.

The journey toward the center of my existence, my own meaning and purpose — not my father's, not anyone else's — had found its way here.

T he sky was an overcast concrete roof with no curves and the sea an equal grey expanse beneath. I could still make errors of inattention, the ones that come most easily near the end, when you begin to think you've made it, and there is still further to go.

Don't get lax with the safety harness just because you smell land.

I added periodic entries on the tape and kept writing. Feo moved calmly on beneath this impenetrable flat sky, at a speed that would bring us to Farallon Light at about 3 a.m., the Loran said. I was talking into the microphone in late afternoon when I could feel my voice take off.

"...Right now! right now!

This whole cover has rolled back in one huge piece from west to east to leave a straight line across the middle of the sky. For the first time in days, the trailing edge of cloud has uncovered the sun and a brilliant, hot, wide, glorious path comes sweeping up at the speed of light, smack dead on the point of the stern and up the mid-line of Feo. The line of sun, brilliant on the white mast and lighting the sail like a flame, is Feo's line from west to east, the course home. The horizon behind us is an impeccable razor's edge all the way behind an immense clearing, pushed back in a moment over thousands of miles, and you see the curvature of the earth along it so clearly you feel yourself perched on the globe itself. The ocean to the east is a marvelous speckled surface, brilliant whitecaps on papal blue, nothing here but us and the hugeness and the change. You're stripped down to yourself and the earth as she truly is, I swear to God it feels..."

It was my own great moment of clearing, I realized much later, etched into that fantastic sky. I had brought myself to it. The journey into fear that asked to be taken for so long had now taken shape in my heart, just as Joe Miller suggested. I felt empowered by the sight of this clearing and the impact of witnessing it, which I could never have imagined in advance, to see the world open up with the horizon sharpened to perfect focus, clarity behind me all around. It was something the moment there alone in the vastness allowed me to take in and possess, a place of clarity that might be mine to apply or draw upon as time went by.

Seas advanced from the north like windowless two-story houses under a wet grey sky. A cold, biting wind topped 30 knots in gusts, with visibility dwindling as rain squalls came and went. It was day 24 now. Black pitched roofs worked their way under Feo's quarter with impassive aggression and shot her down one steep rolling slope after another. She seemed to grow small in each trough as I looked back up at the wall of water looming at three or four times our height. With the pressure of the wind and the angular velocity of these seas, elements for which she had been bred urging her on, Feo thrived.

In the cold and dark oncoming rain I was afraid to sleep again until we got safely to the dock. A freighter that had materialized at close range in the early evening a few nights before still had me looking over my shoulder. It went across our stern at an oblique angle to the west, black steel on grey foam with a faint white command tower aft. If Feo had been a half-hour earlier to the spot, we might have converged. Just a few hours earlier, radio reports logged a collision between the aircraft carrier Eisenhower and an ocean freighter off Virginia. No lives lost.

The return waypoints were all programmed into the Loran — the approach buoys and inner markers of Bonita Point Light, the Golden Gate tower, Alcatraz and Pier 39 itself — and the alarm was set to go off as soon as we reached within five miles of the Farallon tower. But my last few fixes had not been confirmed by the Loran, which meant that one of us — machine or human — was wrong about how far away the Farallon Light might be. This was a price of solo sailing, when you would give your arm to get another opinion about what you were doing, or just have another set of eyes.

The night swirled thick with rain and fog, the seas running eight to ten feet. Feo pounded along as the Loran screen proclaimed a shrinking distance all the way — ten miles, eight miles, seven, six. I expected the tower to loom in the mist well before we got close. She was charging ahead on a broad reach under a double reef, the seas pitching her forward with a rush and I was hand-steering, watching for the light I knew must be there.

A mile and a half.

Foam thundered from her bow. Harnessed into the cockpit after nearly 30 hours without sleep, I was now fighting to stay warm, wet through a rip in the seat of my foul weather gear that happened during a fall when a sea caught us unexpectedly from behind and the harness caught me within inches of going over the side.

She kept closing, no sign of a light and we only had to be off by a few hundred yards to the north to find Noonday Rock the hard way.

Three-quarters of a mile.

This was all happening faster than I expected. After weeks with nothing in sight the invisible coast seem to be charging at us on its own. *The alarm never sounded.*

Now in the faint cabin light the Loran proclaimed us within four-tenths of a mile and as Feo rushed toward the wall of black I tried to calculate how many yards four-tenths of a mile really is *4/10 of 5,000 is two thousand feet which is less than seven hundred yards* and then I wondered exactly where on the island that light was located. I had not programmed the Loran to allow for land between the light and us.

The Loran means total distance to the tower, not to the near shore!

I shot below with a panicked sense of Feo closing at top speed whether I was ready or not, the coastal current running swiftly from left to right as we came on. Down below on the chart I could see the light tower was on the far side of the island by several hundred yards. No time to measure now. Whatever safe distance we had left — if the Loran was not fabricating this out of some bogus signal — was occupied partly by the island. Only .3 miles *a third of 5,200 is 1,600 feet or 500 yards or so* and up in the cockpit all I could see was all black and slanted rain under the masthead light.

OW-WOO!

A chilling sound, a man's call? Humans shouting off to the left?! *Could someone see us?*

OW! OW-OW-OW-OOO!

Was that a ship or freighter light up over the bow?

OW-OW-ARR-ARR! and then it hit me — sea lions on the Farallons or maybe Noonday Rock if we were approaching from the wrong angle. The noise of their barking, animal warning where the machine failed, was carrying across.

Jesus Christ, how close did you have to be to hear them like this?

I yanked Feo sharply to starboard, fearful of jibing her over, but far enough to buy a few hundred yards straight across the island's face, and then faintly

maybe it was there and maybe it was only imagination

thrusting up into the night, *because if not I had no idea what these signals could mean*

a light — a vague spread of luminous rain, now gone.

I pressed Feo's bow further downwind to her limit, my body trembling with cold and fear of imminent collision, ready to spin her across in front of that whistling breeze to jibe out of danger no matter what the damage to the rigging might be in these gusts, and the barking was louder

ARW-ARW-ARW! when just off to port and pulling abeam that cacophony of raucous laughter rattled across the water.

We must be safely by.

Unless!

I fastened the wheel and jumped below to the chart table. *Yes there is another rock downwind in our path if we are within 100 yards of the big island!*

Ears pricked like an animal's ahead for anything, binoculars no good staring into nothing when something like a shadow rose just off to port, a thickening in the dark. Something on its own or a rock etched out of my fear, maybe a boat or shape of a rock and now I was sure, a rock without sound, no seals here.

It loomed like a hill along a moonless country road, shape and mass and motionlessness ghosting by close enough to smell the stench of guano, a sudden surge of whispering around the great rock's flanks as we slipped past and into deep water again, just 15 miles of open water left to the Gate, almost all down-wind.

San Francisco rose out of her own mist with the dawn behind her, a photograph rendered in early morning orange monochrome. Alcatraz lay as a silent monolith against the Oakland hills, imitation freighter carved in stone with an abandoned prison for a pilothouse. North Beach climbed in repetitive pale building blocks toward the Transamerica Pyramid, spiked center of a clock and I could see street canyons cross-hatched at dark right angles like a distant map face, a mysterious configuration of time and place. She was still asleep and for this brief stretch before she woke I had her to myself.

Feo moved with the worn motion of an exhausted mount, pointing herself toward the outward jutting of windowed timber that was the Pier. I felt woven into her familiar spars and deck lines and sails, which flapped tiredly downwind across this last stretch. Rounding the breakwater toward F-dock, and re-entering the slip where I had first come aboard brought back vivid flashes — Michel's hand-twisted cigarettes, the unfamiliar sounds in the rigging as Feo began to feel like mine. A woman who had been varnishing an adjacent boat had appeared one morning to give me a tattered copy of Moitessier's "The Long Way." She recognized Feo as a twin of the Frenchman's famous Joshua and said that this boat could take me places I might have only imagined. The woman's name was Faith. A few nights later, approaching the pier alone, I had my first vague apprehension of a book about Feo becoming real as an ocean passage might. I pictured Brody and telling him about getting sick and meeting Joe Miller, who quoted someone I didn't recognize: "As a man thinketh in his heart, so is he. Faith is the substance of things hoped for and the evidence of things unseen." He got me to utter those words *"in the path of my fear."* I was just stepping out of the car and those mysterious tears rushed out of my eyes. A woman dodged me near the sidewalk, startled at this strange man, raincoat slung over his shoulder and muttering to himself, rubbing at his face with one hand as he dashed through the traffic, listening to the voice in him saying *this is what you have to do.* How I had sat in Feo's cockpit the next day, looking up at North Beach, feeling that in some way my life had just begun. When I told Brody this, he said, you'll get there, and I said, *I know.* These moments all converged to point here, and now they seemed to point further on.

❀

Years before, when I professed to that newspaper colleague that I couldn't write my first book until my father died, the reasons were a mystery to me. So what had happened? I had taken my own advice, which Joe Miller had first elicited, combining the logic of the children's story about the dwarf — walk toward that thing you fear and it may not be there when you arrive — and my own words later on. Following the path of my fear and trying to live closer to my own heart, I discovered something of my father I had lost long ago, or something in myself I could not admit, or had hidden because it had been driven into hiding. He had come along with me into the ocean after all, not physically as I might have hoped but in a way I could never have imagined, where I came to see him with changed eyes. Perhaps I had taken too long to come to this point, to shed old fantasies, to begin to abandon a child's rage with his father — to see the man behind the authority, however he wielded it.

And when I first told him that I had decided to leave the newspaper to work full time on a book about sailing, he wanted to know why anyone would want to read about sailing alone to Hawaii and back.

"People sail to Hawaii all the time," he said. "Besides, it's pretty risky to leave an established job with the economy headed for hell in a hand basket." He had been reading about the rise of the markets in Japan and was sure the coming collapse would pull down the developed economies.

"It's certainly not a choice I could ever have made," he said.

"No," I said. "I suppose not."

We fell silent again. The reflected mast of Enfin pointed like a compass needle directly across the still water at us. However much he had ever stood in my way, he had taught me so many things that would serve me forever. He was never happier than when he was on a boat, nor gentler to those around him. Our time together on the water had been one of his most important gifts, that of shared experience and the wisdom that comes with practice. He had loaned me the money to buy Feo when no bank would do it. He sent me off for Hawaii with gifts of a sextant, his precious Director course plotter, the taffrail log — all the basic tools I needed to find my way. And the trip had liberated me from certain limitations, to begin to see him more clearly as a man, as I began to see myself.

He was still here, with my mother, for better or worse, in the place of our origins. I felt ineffably bound to him in blood and love, and distinct from him in ways I had not before. Motionless together on that porch, we might have been a couple of sailors on the prow of an old ship, locked in twilight together, watching the night come gently down.

I saw his death approaching and in the night ocean the blackness that would be the void. It struck me then that by as much as the universe is indifferent, by that much do we possess it. By denying nothing it invites everything. Life brings us to the point beyond which we must take ourselves.

I had hoped to finish the book before he died, but I was not able to do it before heart disease and old age finally overtook him. More than a year after I left the newspaper to write the book, which I had given myself one year to do, he was hospitalized again in Lowell, and I feared he might go at any time. So I came east to see him and showed him an early draft that was being circulated to New York publishers, and which I thought might find its way into print — my mistake in more ways than one. It would not be done for another 15 years.

"So." He looked at me with narrowed eyes, and I was conscious that so late in the day he was still in his bathrobe. "You hate me, then?"

It was a statement only half-meant as a question. I saw him hunched in their kitchen, forlornly, my mother poised somewhere nearby in the house, listening. I will always be able to picture that grim pain on his face, a distance in his eyes, a rebuke to me but also the pain of injury coming from a greater depth. He was a prisoner and victim of himself in some ways, which I came to understand over time — one who perceived demons in himself and let them obliterate the angels. That was his trap and he flung it at me as if it were my own.

"No," I said. "I meant the book to be about love, and things that happen along the way. But you will have to see it for yourself, if you can."

I wish in that moment that I had acknowledged all the things he had done to get me there — schools and skiing and tennis and wood-carving and shooting, so much more than just the sailing — and how much I appreciated him for all of that. But I couldn't say that, or anything else. I felt undercut, unhinged that he should have seen only hatred in my story of time alone at sea and the conflicts of my growing up and my own effort to cover the vast reaches between us.

We never spoke of it again. The changes I made to the manuscript after he died were mostly to the end. We scattered a third of his ashes in Penobscot Bay, and buried another third in Massachusetts in a graveyard across from the Dunstable Little League field. The last third I would scatter in Ganges Harbor off Saltspring Island, accompanied by Emily and his two surviving brothers. It was then I reserved a few remaining ashes in the arbutus box to store aboard Feo in case we ever made it to Cape Horn.

Epilogue

It was springtime in Arizona, 18 years after I brought Feo back into the slip — or she brought me — and a marriage and a half later. I was on the brink of another rupture I had hoped never to repeat, this more than 15 years since my father's death. A therapist had encouraged me to spend a month in an Arizona treatment center specializing in depressives and alcoholics and people seething over something. Try to get at the bottom of my anger, she said, and the sadness that drove me to seek solace however I might find it. At Cottonwood the clinicians diagnosed me with a particular brand of depression — a lifelong melancholic, if you translated the science into a more romantic term — and not an alcoholic, clinically speaking, just someone who had learned to manage the effects of early violence with liquor, among other stimulants. Sailing into the ocean alone might have been the most important one, and the propensity for falling in love, but not staying that way, a close second.

In a small room I was asked to watch a series of small light impulses on a screen, listen to a related tone through a headset and feel a concurrent vibration through a pair of nodes attached to my thighs. This process, known as EMDR, had been invented by a graduate student to help Vietnam veterans come to terms with their most troubling memories. It was thought to work on the part of the brain that holds emotional memory in the exact form in which it was experienced, and somehow reliving the emotional content would lessen its impact over time.

The clinician began by asking me to visualize the earliest and most violent scenes of my childhood. As I would later explain — when I was able to speak again — the scene unfolded with an eerie self-edited quality. The eye of the camera could see my bedroom door open inward. It could see my father taking off his jacket, but it could only hear sounds after that, a small voice rising and the sound of the rubber hose in the air, and several impacts on flesh. It could not see anything anymore. I was aware of a violent contraction in my lower chest or stomach as if my insides were trying to solidify and exit through my throat. I was aware of that noise, perhaps a human voice — not a moan nor a cry and not a sound I had ever heard, a keening, something emanating from a point just in front of the base of my spine. Later I would say it felt like trying to vomit a truck, or disgorge an animal twice my size, the thing that had long threatened to kill me if I ever let it out, and the violence of it shocked me. I felt my chest cavity had been occupied by a glass vase, wide almost to my shoulders at the top, narrowing to my groin, filled with a brownish liquid that was viscous on the surface but thickened as it went down to solidify at the narrow bottom. I vomited most of it out on waves of sound and violent heaving but no effort would dislodge the last few inches of clot at the bottom, under which I could see clear glass. Under that was something original, a place I might have existed in pure form before anyone or anything so clouded my experience. The sound pulled me out of my chair and down onto the floor into the position of a man crouched and curled on his side, retching until he ran out of oxygen, which took a surprisingly long time.

"What did the camera see when you turned it on your-self?" the clinician asked. He had not moved, waiting for me to be still, which must have taken five or ten minutes, though I had no accurate sense of time.

"Nothing," I said. "It was as if a cone covered that part of the room, between the two beds. The camera could not see me."

"Why the cone, do you think?" he asked.

"I don't know."

"It's pretty clear to me," he said. "You learned to protect yourself a long time ago. No one gets in there now, not even you."

So Don Michael, my old mentor and friend who coined the phrase and suggested I pay attention to "the fathers you find," had been right. A child cannot reconcile violence at the hands of one who is supposed to love him, and whom he loves without condition, before any of us learns to put language on feeling. It cannot make sense to the child unless he is deserving of the violence and the pain and the anger behind it. How could that be? And in what form would the confusion reside over time, along with the shame and humiliation that he took in without words, and how might these be expressed?

Without that time alone in the ocean — and the interven-ing years, in which my brother brought about his own injury and I became the oldest male in our family, and my mother died, as I struggled to get back to the story and found my way to Cottonwood, and afterwards — I could not have come to this final point. Perhaps with the right time and distance, if these are required, a man can reconcile what a child cannot, and choose to let it go, like ashes to the deep. What deeds he had done I could acknowledge as my father's alone — never to be approved but no longer in possession of me, as I might choose to let them go. This was forgiveness. Who could ever know what brought him there, who taught him that the violence was the right thing to do with his own children? He must have been shown it by someone before he had any idea what it meant. He must have seen it play out in his four younger brothers. My own brother, loyal to authority at all costs, would never speak to me of his experience at our father's hands, but his wife had once said to mine that my brother's had been far worse than either sibling afterwards. Did it matter? My brother had grown up as a willful perfectionist, a natural leader, a team captain and leading stage actor in his college dramatic society, and eventually a Wall Street litigator known to be inexhaustible and deadly cool under pressure. From his days at Yale in the Silliman House, his early adventures aboard a freighter to Rio and years teaching at the American University of Beirut, where his closest friends worked in intelligence, and from his years at the University of Virginia, and proximity to Washington, DC, I became convinced he was a spy, something he never conceded nor convincingly denied. Still he had the aloofness and control that you would wish to have in an agent if not your own brother. If he ever lost control, I only ever saw it happen within the family — ours or his — it always took the form of rage. Maybe this partly explained why at 52-years-old a prominent Manhattan attorney in otherwise excellent shape felt the need to bench-press 400 pounds, because whatever point he had come to wasn't quite good enough. And somehow he breathed wrong and blew up the carotid artery at the base of his skull, bringing on a stroke that would cripple him permanently. The brother who taught me to throw left-handed because "it will make you unhittable," he said (something that Little League quickly disproved), who had magical accuracy in his own throwing arm and the guts to go after the town bullies on my behalf, who had taught me on the strength of his own, never-once-mentioned experience to face my father down with passive silence, would spend the waning years of his life confined to bed, growing slightly more speechless day by day. I would never know if the worst in my father had destroyed the best of my brother, who had been and would always remain such a hero to me.

We can never know everything, in ourselves or others. And yet it was all in us, the grief and the joy, the devils and the angels, if they could ever be discerned for what they were and put in their proper place, if the pieces would ever fit, if we only knew which ones to bring together to form the truth that mattered. My father had given me so much to carry through life — even the ability I never asked for, to swallow pain and to hold back tears, no matter what — and it was now up to me to decide what to carry on. By forgiving him his violence I did not need to approve it, I only needed to let it go. Sailing alone to Hawaii, at a time when I knew I had to do something, and his gifts were still required, had taken me far enough away from him, and brought me back close enough, to see into the deep of my family life and begin to work my way toward some answers. One was to release the ashes at last, forever, into my father's wake.

Glossary

Backstays – the wires that run from the top of the mast aft toward the stern.

Boom – the spar that holds the bottom edge of a sail and keeps the sail in tension against the wind.

Bow pulpit – a lookout position or enclosed area built above the bowsprit.

Bowsprit – a projection built beyond the foremost section of the deck that allows a sailboat to carry larger jibs or headsails forward of the mast.

Bulkhead – a wall or partition separating sections of a boat below decks.

Cockpit – the portion of the deck recessed for crew and passengers.

Combers – a term referring to large and often breaking waves.

Companionway – the ladder or stairway from the cockpit down below, or from one deck to another.

Cross-tree/spreader – See diagram. The portion of the spars that "spread" the stays (rigging wires) as they descend from the top of the mast to the deck. Also called "cross-trees" because of their t-shaped appearance on the mast.

Dead reckoning – The process of recording speed, distance and course, allowing for wind and current effects, to calculate your current position.

Fix – when used in navigation, a word noting the point of location determined by coordinate lines on a chart.

Gimbals – a device that allows an object to rotate on a single axis. In pairs, these can allow a lamp or compass to remain level while a boat is moving violently in one direction or another.

Gunwales – the edges of the hull where the deck meets the sides of the vessel (taken from the place where you would rest your rifle to take aim).

Halyard – The line or rope that hoists a sail up or lowers it down.

Hatch – the cover or horizontal "door" over an opening that leads down below decks.

Heave to – the process of deliberately stalling a sailboat in a nearly upwind position by trimming the headsail (jib or staysail) to windward and trimming the mainsail at close to dead center. By lashing the steering to force the boat upwind, it will be held in a stalled position by the opposing pressure of the two sails. ("Hove to" is the past tense of the verb." A hardy vessel in a hove to position can endure very rough conditions while minimizing discomfort for those below.

Heel – a term referring to a sailboat's natural tendency to lean over under the pressure of the wind, as in "The boat heeled to starboard as the wind increased." How much a boat heels under a given amount of wind pressure depends on its ballast and hull design.

Hull – the body of the vessel, which in Feo's case is 39 feet 11 inches in overall length and 12.5 feet in width, or "beam".

In irons – a term describing the "stuck" position facing upwind where a sailboat cannot turn in either direction because of the wind pressure on both sides of the sail.

Jib – a smaller sail forward of the main mast.

Jibe – the maneuver when a sailing vessel going downwind changes direction and causes the sail to cross from one side of the vessel to the other. Also "gybe." This maneuver can be dangerous in high winds and stressful on the rig.

Ketch – a two-masted sailboat in which the main mast is mounted somewhat forward of the beam and the smaller (mizzen) mast is mounted forward of the rudder.

Knot – a unit of speed meaning one nautical mile per hour = roughly 1.151 mph.

Leeward – the downwind side of a vessel.

Leeway – the sideways progress that any sailboat makes as the wind pushes it "across" its direction of travel. Therefore a vessel sailing north in a westerly wind will always make some easterly "slippage" as it goes north, also referred to as its "set and drift." Over long distances, the "leeway" can bring a boat far off course and must therefore be carefully taken into account by the navigator.

Loran – a term referring to the "Long Range Navigation" system in which unique signals transmitted from shore allow a navigator to calculate his position.

Luff up – turning up into the wind (causing the sail to shake or "luff"). This takes pressure off the sail and allows the boat to straighten up even in very high winds.

Main – a term often used to refer to the "mainsail," or largest sail in the ketch configuration.

Mizzen – a term referring to the smaller mast in a ketch rig.

Port – the left side of the boat when facing forward.

Reef – a term for reducing sail area, as in, "Fearing higher winds, he put a reef in the sail." "Reefing gear" may refer to the lines and sail attachments that permit the sail to be reduced and lashed to the boom.

Rhumb-line – a straight line.

Rigging – the wires or ropes used to support the masts.

Scuppers – the area along the edge of the deck where water collects and is sluiced overboard.

Set and drift – the effect on a boat of sideways current or wind pressure that cause it to move off its intended course or track toward its destination.

Sheet – a term referring to a rope or line that is used to secure or trim a sail against the pressure of the wind.

Sister-ship – a vessel of the same design. Feo's hull specifications, weight and configuration match that of Bernard Moitessier's 1961 "Joshua," in which he led the fleet in the world's first single-handed round-the-world race.

Skeg – a word denoting the fin or blade that serves underwater as a steering rudder or small keel, common to sailing self-steering apparatus and surfboards, for example.

Sloop – a sailing rig with a single mast, which is stepped slightly forward of the center of the hull.

Spar – a word referring to the mast (the vertical support for the sail), or a boom (the horizontal support for the sail).

Stanchions – vertical fixtures along the edge of the deck that hold lifelines to help keep sailors from falling overboard.

Stay – The wire or "shroud" attached to a mast at various heights from the masthead down to the gunwale or "chainplates" to support the mast.

Staysail – an intermediate sail between the mainmast and the leading jib.

Starboard – the right side of the boat when facing forward.

Taffrail log – an overboard device for measuring distance while moving through the water.

Telltale – device that shows the direction of the wind.

Tiller – a means of steering a boat in which the tiller attaches to the rudder and is usually handled in the cockpit. In Feo's case, the tiller is attached by cables to the steering wheel in the cockpit.

Windlass – a mechanical device used for hoisting or lowering the anchor or for performing other mechanical tasks involving rope or chain.

Williwaw – Accelerating winds that come down off high ground to strike the water close offshore.

Zephyrs – small or faint movements of wind.

Feo

Feo was constructed of steel by Meta Shipyards in Tarare, France in 1969, a sistership to the famous "Joshua" that Jean Knocker designed for (and with) Bernard Moitessier, who sailed in the first single-handed "Golden Globe" round-the-world race in 1968. Feo is 47-feet overall in length (39-feet 11-inches stem-to-stern on the deck), with a draft (depth below the waterline) of 5.5 feet and a beam (width) of 12.5 feet. Ketch-rigged (with a second, smaller mast located ahead of the tiller), Feo weighs 13 gross tons and with a full keel is known for relative stability in heavy weather, or "sea-kindliness." Her hull and deck are steel, mast and booms are wood. She is designed for single-handed sailing, with a small, self-bailing cockpit and lines that lead into the helmsman's area. With a full galley and refrigeration, one head (toilet) and shower, she sleeps two aft, two forward and two amidships. She is powered by a single inboard diesel engine.

1	Bobstay	9	Topping Lift
2	Windlass	10	Cockpit area
3	Forestay	11	Winch
4	Jib	12	Mizzen-mast
5	Staysail	13	Cross-tree/spreader
6	Main-mast	14	Jigger
7	Telltale	15	Windvane
8	Mainsail		

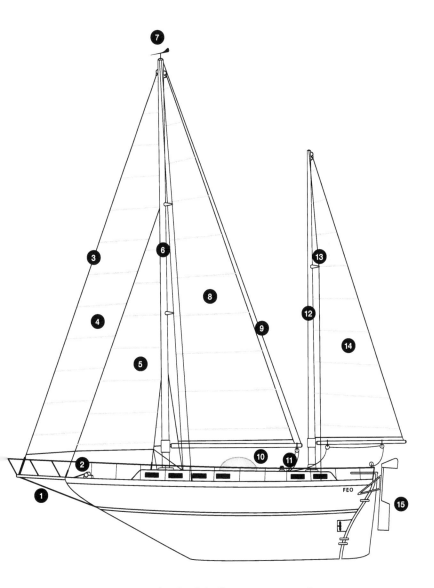

Not in complete detail, for illustration purposes only.

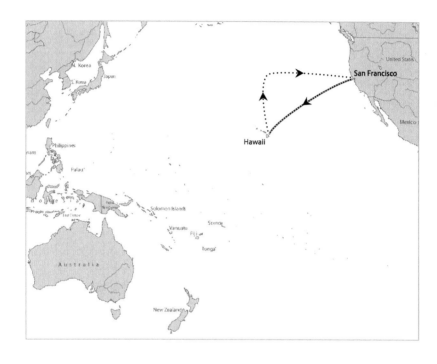

Route from San Francisco to Hawaii and back

Course and positions approximated

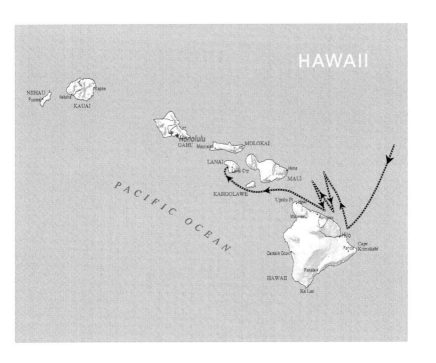

Finding My Way Into Hawaii...

Course and positions approximated

About the author

Eric Best began his sailing life in Maine's Penobscot Bay, racing and cruising with his father along the New England coast. En route to a distinguished career as a journalist, he attended the 1972–3 Stanford Graduate Program in Creative Writing and won a 1982–3 Neiman Fellowship for journalists at Harvard. He pursued his passion for sailing with two solo trips from San Francisco to Hawaii and back and spent a decade living aboard Feo in the San Francisco Bay. He raced Feo from Newport-Bermuda in 2002 before skippering his 65-foot Swan from San Francisco to Jamaica in 2005. He is also author of a children's book and animated film, "The Deep" (whatcouldpossiblybe.com). Eric lives in Brooklyn with his three children.

*"Ready am I to go, and my eagerness with sails full set
awaits the wind.*

*Only another breath will I breathe in this still air,
only another loving look cast backward,*

*And then I shall stand among you,
a seafarer among seafarers."*

Khalil Gibran
The Prophet

7618731R0

Made in the USA
Charleston, SC
24 March 2011